A 1980s
CHILDHOOD

A 1980s CHILDHOOD

FROM HE-MAN TO SHELL SUITS

MICHAEL A. JOHNSON

To Rachel, Amelia and Isabel

Front cover image: © Getty Images
Back cover image: *top*: © Lifetouch/Wikimedia Commons

First published 2012

The History Press
The Mill, Brimscombe Port
Stroud, Gloucestershire, GL5 2QG
www.thehistorypress.co.uk

British Library Cataloguing in Publication Data.
A catalogue record for this book is available from the British Library.

ISBN 978 0 7524 6337 7

Typesetting and origination by The History Press
Printed in Great Britain
Manufacturing managed by Jellyfish Print Solutions Ltd

Contents

ACKNOWLEDGEMENTS

With thanks to all those who have kindly supported me with feedback, memories and advice, as well as enduring months of me waffling on about eighties trivia. Special thanks to the following people who have kindly given permission for me to use their photos to illustrate this book: Bill Bertram, Sharon Emerson, Rebecca Güreci, Ian Falconer, Darian Hildebrand, Jim Lane, Alan Light, Grant Mitchell, Helge Øverås, Thomas Uhlemann, Christos Vittoratos, Franny Wentzel, David Wright, www.allaboutapple.com, along with Wikimedia/Wikipedia users: Charles01, Evan-Amos, Hubersparge, Lifetouch, MartinLing, OSX, Schlaier, Squelle and ThePassenger.

All other photographs are from my own personal collection and were taken by either me or my dad, David Johnson. Thanks to my two brothers Alan and Martin for letting me share these potentially embarrassing photos with the whole world! Thanks also to the community of nostalgia fans at www.DoYouRemember.co.uk who helped with my research and a big thanks to my friend Rebecca Güreci, for proofreading, encouraging me and providing a source of inspiration for the chapter on eighties fashion.

Special thanks to Kirsty Spence for providing editorial.

While every reasonable care has been taken to avoid any copyright infringements, should any valid issues arise then I will look to correct them in subsequent editions.

One

INTRODUCTION

Usually, the introduction to a book like this would include some kind of preamble giving an overview of the political and socio-economic developments of the 1980s, perhaps comparing how radically different the decade was from the seventies and summarising how the eighties came to influence life in the nineties and beyond. There may also be some sort of tedious discussion regarding the state of foreign affairs, industry, commerce and finance, along with some dates and figures presented in a neat chart. There may even be a pie chart or a Venn diagram.

But this is not that sort of book. There are no pie charts to be found here, and definitely no Venn diagrams. If you want hard facts, analysis and political commentary then you've bought the wrong book. If you want a light-hearted stroll down memory lane filled with frivolous comments and juvenile banter, rejoice! This is the book you've been looking for.

This is a book about the 1980s the way I saw it when I was there, busy being a kid. It's a collection of the things I remember best about the eighties through the eyes of a child who was 3 years old when the decade began and 13 years old when it ended; a child who laughed at the Spitting Image puppets because they had funny faces, not because I understood the political satire. Within these pages you'll be transported back to a time when shell suits were cool, Dave Lee Travis was the hairy face of Radio One and *Agadoo* was number two in the charts; a time when the must-have Christmas present was a Big Trak or a Rubik's Cube, and a time when white dog poos littered the streets like confetti.

This book is an unashamedly biased collection of the things that I remember, the way I remember them and, because there's nowhere near enough space for me to catalogue *everything* from the eighties, I've selected the things that I found most memorable or meant something special to me.

Now I like to think that I had a fairly normal child-hood, except for that whole third nipple thing, and so I suspect that my recollections of childhood in the eight-ies are going to be pretty similar to those of most other people who grew up in that era. If you're a child of the eighties yourself, you're probably going to remember most of the same stuff as me and will be doing a lot of nodding, grinning and cringing as you read through some of the memories that we share. If you were an adult in the eighties, well, chances are you'll still remember the same stuff, but you might not be able to identify as easily with wearing He-Man picture pyjamas or trying to play the theme tune to *The Flumps* on your school recorder. Of course, if you weren't even born in the eighties, then you're about to learn just how many cool things you missed out on.

I suppose it might be useful if I share a little bit of background about who I am and where I came from before we get on with things. My name is Michael Johnson and I was born in 1977 at Bournemouth Hospital in Dorset. I was the second of three noisy and excitable blonde-haired little boys and, along with our mum and dad, three cats and a dog, we all lived happily together in a bungalow in a quiet residential area just outside the market town of Wimborne Minster.

Given that I was only 3 years old in January 1980, I'm a bit too young to have any interesting memories of the seventies (unless you consider my memory of doing a poo on the floor behind the sofa as interesting), but rather conveniently for the purposes of writing a book about the eighties, my memory started to function pretty well from 1980 onwards. In fact, I have one of those memories that is great at storing useless trivia from the past and, for some reason, I can more easily remember the registration plate of my dad's Datsun Bluebird from twenty-five years ago than I can remember what I was doing this time yesterday.

This bizarre memory for nostalgic trivia came in very handy in 2004 when I launched a retro website called

Me eating a Wall's Funny Feet ice cream in the garden at home in 1986.
(Author's Collection)

www.DoYouRemember.co.uk which attempted to cat-alogue pretty much everything I could remember from the eighties into a series of neatly arranged articles. In fact, I got so carried away with the project that I decided to include everything I remembered from the nine-ties as well, and also began researching the seventies for good measure. Well, to cut a long story short, the website became hugely popular and I found myself filling my brain with even more eighties trivia and am now a kind of virtual museum curator of a glorious online museum of eighties antiquities.

I am also the married father of two little girls who tolerate my passion for eighties pop culture and who occasionally join me in watching reruns of *Back to the Future* or old episodes of *Fraggle Rock* on YouTube, never mocking me when I wear my *A-Team* t-shirt and always ignoring me when I tell them that the music today isn't a patch on the music of the eighties.

So anyway, that's enough about me; time for some eighties big hair and legwarmers as we dive headlong into the embarrassing world of eighties fashion. Enjoy!

Two

FASHION

At the stroke of midnight on 31 December 1979, millions of people joyously celebrated the end of the 1970s and the arrival of the 1980s. At the precise moment Big Ben tolled for midnight, every man around the world ripped off his flared trousers and his platform shoes, slipped on a pair of grey, flecked trousers, a pastel-coloured pair of espadrilles and rolled up the sleeves of his beige jacket. Meanwhile, the womenfolk used a variety of household objects to improvise shoulder pads in their tops and then cut the fingers off their lace gloves before stepping into some pink legwarmers.

The only people who didn't take part in this synchronised global fashion shift were the Chinese, whose new year didn't start until a few weeks later, and the French, who are always a few years behind.

Sadly, it would take a few months before the mullets and big hair would appear and in the first quarter of the year the hairdressing industry nearly collapsed as the entire nation started growing their hair long. The industry was only saved by a sudden and unprecedented demand for hairspray.

Well OK, I've exaggerated that slightly, but there really was an explosion in the pace of fashion shifts in the early eighties, largely driven by the ever-increasing influence of pop culture. Music and movies had certainly had an impact on the fashion trends of previous decades, but it wasn't until the eighties that it really gathered momentum to the point where virtually all fashion trends were now inspired by pop stars, TV shows or movies.

When Madonna burst on to the music scene in 1983 her outrageous dress sense caused a sensation which inspired as many as it outraged. Madonna was certainly to blame for a sharp increase in the number of horrified fathers telling their daughters, 'You're not going out dressed like that!'

In the early days, Madonna often wore short skirts over leggings with fishnet gloves, rubber bracelets, bows in her messy, bleached-blonde hair (with dark roots), as well as headbands, long strings of beads and lace ribbons. But as she moved into her 'Like a Virgin' phase, she clearly felt that her accessories were the most important part of her outfit and began ditching her clothing, bit by bit, until she was left in just her underwear along with some long lace gloves, a few bracelets and a Boy Toy belt. Alarmingly for parents, this actually inspired many young girls to start wearing bustiers or brassieres as outer garments, often accompanied by some large crucifix necklaces.

While this particular fashion trend was fairly extreme and limited mainly to attention-seekers, Madonna's influence was widespread and women of all ages began wearing short, tight, lycra miniskirts and tubular dresses, along with bolero-style jackets and lace gloves, often with the fingers chopped off. As for the new trend of wearing legwarmers as a fashion accessory, we can't blame Madonna this time, but pop culture is guilty again with inspiration inevitably drawn from the new genre of dance films such as *Fame* (1980), *Flashdance* (1983), *Footloose* (1984) and *Dirty Dancing* (1987). Around the time *Flashdance* hit the box offices, teenage girls around the world that had never previously been interested in dance started buying legwarmers to wear over their leggings, jeans or tights.

Flashdance also gave rise to the ripped sweatshirt look that turned an ordinary grey sweatshirt into a fashion classic. Jennifer Beals, the lead actress in *Flashdance*, famously wore a grey sweatshirt with a large neck hole on the poster advertising the film and the large neck hole meant that the sweatshirt could slip down to show one bare shoulder. This was a fairly easy do-it-yourself fashion and many perfectly good sweatshirts were ripped up to emulate the look. Apparently, Beals said that the ripped sweatshirt look was a complete accident and came about when her sweatshirt shrank in the wash and she had to cut a large hole at the top so she could get it on again. Sounds a little unlikely to me, since the sweatshirt looked extremely baggy and I don't remember her head being especially oversized. A close cousin of the *Flashdance* sweatshirt was the Batwing jumper, which took the bagginess of the grey sweater and accentuated the effect under the arms to create a garment that looked like it might have the aerodynamic properties required for freefall gliding.

This new fashion of wearing sports clothing as casual clothing was partly inspired by the dance films and partly by the rather random eighties craze for aerobics. For some reason, the world went aerobics crazy in the mid-1980s with vast numbers of women (and men) buying Jane Fonda workout videos. In the UK we were treated to daily doses of the Green Goddess, who was clearly made of rubber, stretching and prancing about on BBC1's *Breakfast Time* almost every day between 1983 and 1987.

If you were a child in the eighties there's a pretty good chance you will remember the shameful sight of your mum standing in front of the telly, probably still in her nightie and without her make-up on, trying in vain to keep up with the Green Goddess as she danced effortlessly around the studio shouting words of encouragement to the viewers at home. You may also remember seeing women dressed in full aerobic outfits, often in neon colours, out walking the dog or doing the shopping. Olivia Newton-John didn't help matters with her music video to *Let's Get Physical*, which featured her dancing around in legwarmers, sweatbands and all the rest of it while doing aerobics with a bunch of sweaty, drooling men. But it wasn't long before this bizarre fashion got out of hand and a new trend evolved in the form of nylon waterproof trousers and matching jacket – the shell suit. Originally designed as outdoor sports-wear, people (who obviously were not doing any sports) started wearing them out everywhere they went.

Shell suits really hit it off in the mid-1980s and it was around that time that fluorescent materials were at the peak of their popularity. This meant that all manner of garish colours and fluorescent strips were thrown together and it didn't even matter if they clashed; in fact, if they did clash that was all the better! It's an odd fact to get your head around, but the most iconic figure to sport a shell suit in the eighties was probably Jimmy Savile, enjoying a spot in the limelight for a respectable amount of time due to the popularity of *Jim'll Fix It*. It was very rare to spot Jim without his beloved shell suit and infa-mous gold chains. In fact, to his dying day he still loved the swishing sound of his nylon attire and the baggy free-dom that it gave him.

Although various manufacturers created different shell suits, the principle of the design was always basically the same: the lightweight top featured a small, rounded collar with a full zip down the centre; arms were generally puffy and it was preferable to have a shell suit that was slightly too big than have the elasticated wrists riding halfway up the forearm. If you wanted to ride the sleeves up on purpose, though, that was OK. The arms might feature brightly coloured strips down the side of them, and it was also possible to find plenty of jackets with fluorescent arrow-like computer-generated designs down the front.

Of course, unless you wanted it to look like you were just wearing a nylon jacket then you simply had to have the matching bottoms to complete the image. Based on the design of a jogging pant, the loose trousers always featured an elasticated waistband with elastic around the ankles. Team this up with a pair of ultra-white socks and chunky white Reebok or Nike's with the tongue out and you had the look! White sock fear just didn't exist in those days; in fact, Michael Jackson had made it positively fashionable to show off your white socks so it was preferable to hitch your trousers up slightly and puff the bottom of the nylon out like an eighties' Aladdin. The beauty of separates is that you can mix and match, so if you wanted to wear the top with jeans (stonewash only, please) or don the bottoms with a jumper, that was fine too.

Even though a shell suit-donned figure was more likely to be seen browsing the shelves of C&A or John Menzies than tearing around a hurdle track, the shell suit's roots were firmly in the sportswear section. The elasticated waists and forgiving movement of the baggy bottoms were perfect for outdoor activities. Kris Akabusi for one loved them very much as he was able to lunge and run to his heart's content without the fear of chafing.

At the same time that some people were dressed as Madonna and others were dressed as aerobics instructors, another group of people were dressed like characters from *Dallas* or *Dynasty* in a new fashion dubbed 'power

My good friend Rebecca demonstrating a big hair and jumpsuit combo.
Notice the casual confidence that comes from knowing how good you look.
(Rebecca Güreci)

dressing'. Power dressing was characterised by women wearing shoulder pads in their dresses, showing off their ostentatious jewellery and styling their hair to make it as large as possible without it collapsing under its own weight.

The origins of power dressing are fairly clear and can, in large part, be attributed to the American soap opera *Dynasty* which was watched by over 250 million viewers. One of the main characters was played by actress Linda Evans, whose naturally broad shoulders gave the Dynasty costume designer, Nolan Miller, the idea of emphasising them with small shoulder pads. She then decided that every other actress had to be shoulder-padded with even bigger pads to match Linda and consequently the shoulder pad war began.

The shoulder pad became an iconic status symbol that represented both power and wealth, and the size of the shoulder pad seemed to correlate directly with the social status of the wearer. The bigger the shoulder pad, the more money you had, and the eighties was definitely a time for shouting about how much money you had (remember the Harry Enfield character 'Loadsamoney'?). Dresses were available with Velcro shoulder pads that could be removed or replaced with different-sized pads. I wonder whether women carried a range of shoulder pads in their handbag for different social occasions.

I don't want to overanalyse the whole power dressing thing, but there was a lot more to it than just copying the characters from *Dynasty*. The 'equality for women' movement actually had quite a lot to do with it, with women playing an increasingly important role in business but still feeling the need to power dress to gain the respect of their male colleagues. You only have to look at the 1980 film *Nine to Five* with Dolly Parton to get a taste of the sexism, bigotry and chauvinism that was still standard fare in many workplaces for much of the eighties.

I'm sure no one would like to think that Mrs Thatcher in any way inspired their fashion sense, but at that time, Mrs T was a leading example of a very ballsy woman power-dressing to gain respect in the almost entirely male world of politics. There is no doubt that her daily appearances on television dressed in power suits reinforced this particular trend. A more appealing ambassador for power dressing, perhaps, was the Princess of Wales, who had to overcome similar challenges as a member of the royal family, and I think we'd all prefer to think that we got our inspiration from Princess Di than from Mrs T.

Power dressing wasn't such a big thing for men, except for uncool yuppies, although many men still had some padding in their shoulders. Instead, an alternative fashion emerged that was way cooler since it was inspired by the American TV series *Miami Vice*. Leading man Don Johnson teamed expensive Armani jackets with casual t-shirts and a few days' beard growth to create a look that told the world you had plenty of money but were still cool with it. It didn't take long before men everywhere were wearing pastel-coloured t-shirts under their expensive designer jackets (or in most cases, their cheap imitation designer jackets).

Of course, in the eighties, you didn't just wear your (fake) designer jacket the way it was intended; you had to roll the sleeves up if you wanted to be truly cool. Any ideas why? Well, I have a theory about how this particular trend started and, after doing a bit of Googling, I didn't come up with any better ideas so I'm taking this opportunity to formally announce 'Johnson's Theory of Rolled-Up Jacket Sleeves'. We've already established that the 1980s was a time when people liked to show off how much money they had, so an expensive designer jacket was the ideal choice of clothing to let everyone know you had plenty of dosh. But then all the people with no money started wearing cheap, fake designer jackets which meant that nobody could tell that your jacket was the real deal. Real designer jackets have actual working buttons on the sleeves that let you unbutton them and roll them up, whereas cheap, fake jackets just have stitched-on buttons that don't actually do anything. If you don't believe me, go and check your suit jacket now and there's a very strong chance it will have fake buttons on the sleeves, unless it cost you more than £500 (and if it did cost you more than £500 and you have fake buttons, you'll know you've been fleeced). So how do you show the world you have a real designer jacket? You simply unbutton the cuffs and roll up the sleeves of course! Now everyone knows you've got loads of money once more.

I can't discuss eighties fashion without mentioning the New Romantic movement, which led to the

famous, over-the-top make-up and clothing demonstrated by people like Adam Ant and Boy George. New
Romanticism really had its roots in the 1970s punk fashion movement, of which Vivienne Westwood was perhaps
the most notable proponent; but instead of taking its cues
from the grim council estates and the miserable struggles
against social deprivation, the New Romantics celebrated
glamour and partying and all things theatrical. Basically,
the New Romantics were the punks that just liked the
dressing-up bit and weren't so keen on all the anarchy.

The bold and streaky make-up was a clear throwback
to punk, as were some of the outlandish frilled costumes
worn by Adam and his Ants, but things had moved on
and become altogether more glamorous. The pirate look
designed by Vivienne Westwood for Adam and the Ants
is probably the most iconic of the New Romantic outfits, with full-sleeved, frilled buccaneer shirts made from
expensive fabrics, Victorian-era Hussar jackets with gold
braiding and high-waisted, baggy trousers tapering at the
ankle, finished off with a white stripe painted across the
bridge of the nose.

I remember my brother being given a make-up set
one Christmas and my mum helping him paint a white
stripe across his face like Adam Ant so he could dance
around the living room with his plastic guitar singing
along to *Stand and Deliver*. As far as I remember, he didn't
ever go out with the make-up on. In fact, you didn't see
many people dressed in full pirate/dandy highwayman
outfits out doing the shopping, but in the music scene

and nightclubs there was no shortage of flamboyant costumes inspired by the likes of David Bowie, Duran Duran, Ultravox, Spandau Ballet and Culture Club.

A toned-down and more practical version of New Romantic fashion began to appear for the less adventurous folk, starting with small shirt collars worn unfolded for men, excessive use of eyeshadow and blusher for women, and quiff hairstyles for either sex.

While many of the eighties fashions can be classified into their own clearly defined genre, like power dressing, aerobics fashion or New Romanticism, there was a considerable overlap between each and ideas were borrowed, modified and mixed together to create entirely new styles. And while many garments can easily be traced back to their pop culture origins, some trends are harder to source or even categorise. Take, for example, the puffball skirt which became very popular in the mid-1980s, being worn by the Princess of Wales and singers Pepsi and Shirlie, among others. It has echoes of the miniskirts of the sixties, while probably being influenced by the outlandish designs of the New Romantics. Rah-rah skirts were another adaptation of the miniskirt but this time with a sports clothing twist taking inspiration from cheerleaders at sporting events.

One of the most popular items of clothing in the eighties for both men and women were stonewashed jeans or, in fact, any garment made from stonewashed or acid-washed denim. Heavy metal bands and bikers seemed particularly keen on faded denim and sometimes took to splattering bleach on their clothes to add an even more 'distressed' look. Of course, if you were wearing stonewashed jeans, they had to be skinny and often finished off with a pair of gleaming white high-top trainers and some neon socks, preferably in two different colours. Michael J. Fox demonstrates this look in the *Back to the Future* trilogy, although I don't remember him having the neon socks. Come to think of it, maybe the neon socks weren't that cool after all.

The hairstyles that accompanied the clothes are worth a mention too, since the eighties played host to some of the most extreme and ridiculous hairstyles the world has ever known. Starting with undoubtedly the worst hairstyle ever, the mullet was a mainstay of eighties fashion and was proudly sported by such celebrities as Pat Sharp, Limahl and Billy Ray Cyrus. The mullet haircut, as you know, consisted of short hair at the front and sides and long hair at the back.

Early prototype mullet haircuts started appearing as far back as the 1960s with Welsh singer Tom Jones sporting a fine example; in the 1970s David Bowie joined in with his own take on the mullet. However, the mullet did not achieve prominence and popularity until the early 1980s when 'hair bands' like Kajagoogoo and Duran Duran somehow made them acceptable.

I don't know what we called them in the eighties but it certainly wasn't 'mullets' and some mullet websites have given credit to the Beastie Boys for inventing the name in their 1994 song *Mullet Head*. I can imagine a

A fine example of a real-life mullet haircut. This photograph makes me instinctively reach for a pair of scissors. *(Courtesy of Lifetouch/Wikimedia Commons)*

few of the names I might have used personally but it's probably best not to print those. Thankfully, the mullet haircut declined in popularity as the decade drew on and was almost completely eradicated, except in Russia where the mullet still thrives in the wild.

Throughout the eighties, the general idea was to make your hair bigger and bigger, using more and more hairspray until either a) the hair collapsed under its own weight; b) the wearer collapsed under the weight of the hair; or c) the hair spontaneously combusted due to the excessive amounts of flammable hairspray used. A variety of different styles were created to achieve the big hair look from the aforementioned mullet to the glam perms of the *Dynasty* power dressers to the downright ridiculous haircut infamously worn by Mike Score of A Flock of Seagulls. If you fancy a laugh, go and search for '80s big hair' on the web and take a look at some of the pictures. You'll be amused at first and then ashamed as you remember how you had your own hair back in the day. If you were one of the big hair bunch, then I want you to know that you are responsible for ruining the cinema experiences of numerous children in the eighties. We had to try and watch the film through the massive dome of hair of the lady in front and while this was extremely frustrating, it did add a kind of early 3D effect to *Teen Wolf*.

As if you hadn't made your head look ridiculous enough with all this big hair and mullet shenanigans, some bright spark decided to make everyone look stupider still by inventing the Deely Bopper. If you don't

Deely Boppers: the world's most pointless yet successful invention. *(Courtesy of Jim Lane/Wikimedia Commons)*

know it by name, you will certainly know it by sight. The Deely Bopper or Deely Bobber was a plastic headband with a pair of springy bobbles on the end that looked a bit like insect antennae. They came in all shapes and colours, decorated with glitter, shaped as hearts or covered in fur, and for some reason people thought they looked great and were quite happy to be seen wearing them. Apparently, they were invented by an American (that explains it) who was inspired by the 'Killer Bees' costumes on *Saturday Night Live*. Being an entrepreneurial sort of fellow, he knocked up his first batch of Deely Boppers in 1981, which his wife named incidentally, and took them to a street fair in Los Angeles where they sold like hot cakes. After selling the idea to the Ace Novelty Co. in Washington, production was ramped up and within a year of the initial launch sales were estimated at 2 million. To this day, I still haven't figured out what they are for but, judging by their popularity, it seems like everyone else has.

As a child in the 1980s, I showed little interest in fashion and dutifully wore whatever my mother gave me. I couldn't have told you the difference between a rah-rah skirt and a puff ball, and neither would I have cared, but I do remember getting disproportionately excited on one occasion when my mum bought my brother and me a pair of espadrilles each from Wimborne Market. In my mind, espadrilles belong with the *Miami Vice* look, a kind of laid-back cool contrasting the simplicity of cheap and simple shoes and t-shirt with the expense of the designer jacket.

However, on reflection, I don't remember Don Johnson ever slipping on his espadrilles before chasing after the bad guys. Not only would they have been uncomfortable when running any distance, they probably would have fallen apart pretty quickly since the soles were made of a kind of flat jute rope that clearly wasn't designed for durability. Although I was hardly ever involved in police chases, my espadrilles didn't last long at all, but then that was probably because they were cheap imitations bought from 'Pete the Feet' at Wimborne Market.

I also remember being given my very first bum bag and feeling extremely cool wearing it, despite looking like a complete fool and having nothing to put in it anyway. I probably don't need to explain what a bum bag was but if you have somehow managed to erase the traumatic memory of the bum bag from your memory, let me remind you. The bum bag was basically an expansion of the money belt concept that lets you keep your money and keys, or maybe some spare shoulder pads, in a convenient little bag strapped around your waist. Despite its name, it was usually worn at the front for security and ease of access, and was second only in uncoolness to those little money purses you wore on a string around your neck. They were available in an astonishing range of shapes, styles and colours and I remember my sister-in-law investing in an expensive-looking black and white cow-skin bum bag that would have looked great if only it was a handbag. No one, I repeat no one, looks good wearing a bum bag.

The Americans don't call them bum bags, they call them fanny packs. There's nothing funny about that. Stop sniggering, you at the back.

I might not have cared much about fashion back then but I did my best to fit in with all the other kids, although I'm not sure you would believe me if you ever saw what I was wearing. One of my few concessions to fashion was the obligatory neon-coloured slap bracelets that everyone had. They were basically just a strip of convex metal covered in a plastic or material outer that looked a bit like a shoehorn when extended. You slapped it onto your arm and it would instantly wrap around your wrist making a rather unusual shoehorn/bracelet combo.

You might now be starting to form a picture of me back in the eighties. Imagine a blonde, bespectacled little boy (nicknamed 'the Milky Bar kid'), wearing a neon-coloured Ocean Pacific t-shirt, neon shorts, pastel-coloured espadrilles, a bum bag around my waist, a slap bracelet on one wrist and a friendship bracelet on the other. Next to the bracelets was a digital 007 wristwatch that played the James Bond theme tune and a baseball cap on my head with the word 'Bad' on it to go with the various Michael Jackson pin badges I was wearing on my burgundy cardigan. Not a nice picture, is it?

I have looked at a few of the key fashions of the 1980s but there is simply not enough room in this book to cover all of the weird and wonderful trends that emerged in those ten years. Somehow we managed to pack more new fashions into one decade than there were in several of the previous decades combined. The pace of change in fashion accelerated so fast that there was a new fashion born with each new music video and every new film. This was a time when MTV had just hit the television screens and brought a big slice of American pop culture into our homes and it was a time when people had more money to spend on fashion than ever before.

I know I've mocked the fashions of the eighties, and deservedly so, but was it really any worse than the fashions of today? Given a choice between a pair of MC Hammer baggy pants and a pair of today's skinny jeans worn to look like they're falling down, I think I'd go for the baggy pants. And if you're still chuckling at the thought of people wearing shell suits, shoulder pads and slap bracelets, take a moment to cast your mind back a few years and ask yourself what YOU were wearing in the eighties.

Three

MUSIC

These days, I have the radio permanently tuned in to my favourite eighties radio station and would be quite happy if I never listened to anything else again. After all, there were so many hundreds, probably thousands, of amazing records made in the eighties by so many talented musicians that you could never possibly tire of hearing them all. When I listen to the music of the eighties, I'm transported back to my childhood – a time of careless innocence, of fun, laughter and excitement – and I like it there and enjoy going back to visit. Each song brings back a different memory for me, perhaps of a film I watched with my brothers or of a day out with the family when we sang along to a song on the radio together. There's something about the music that stirs the memories and emotions and has the power to take you on a journey back in time and make you feel good all over again. And so, without further ado, I'd like you to join me on a trip down memory lane as I share with you some of the music that brings back my happy memories from the eighties.

Yazz and the Plastic Population

While Yazz actually had four UK top ten hits in the eighties, the one that most people will remember her for is *The Only Way is Up*, the incongruously perky and upbeat song about poverty, degradation and the threat of potential eviction. The song became an instant hit when it was released in 1983 and spent five weeks at number one in the UK charts, ultimately becoming the second biggest selling single of the year.

My mum loved this song and bought the vinyl record so that she could dance around the living room to it, making a refreshing change from her usual Julio Iglesias records. I remember once, on a family day out, we stopped off for lunch at a quaint rural pub in the heart of the Dorset countryside. The pub seemed to be frequented solely by farmers and ruddy-faced old men who eyed us suspiciously as we took our seats. While we waited for our food to be served, my brothers and I decided to liven up the deathly dull atmosphere of the pub by using our pocket money to play *The Only Way is Up* on the jukebox. The silence of the little pub was shattered by the opening horn blast of the song, much to the amusement of me and my brothers. In fact, we found it so amusing that we decided to sacrifice more of our pocket money to play it again and again, much to the disgruntlement of the muttering locals.

Musical Youth

There's a common misconception that Musical Youth's number one hit in 1982, *Pass the Dutchie*, is a song about cannabis, when in fact the song is about extreme poverty; the 'dutchie' in the lyrics refers to a type of pot used for cooking. It's an easy mistake to make though because the song *Pass the Dutchie* is actually a cover version of a song released just one year earlier called *Pass the Koutchie* by the Mighty Diamonds, which was indeed a song all about cannabis. But in 1982 I was only 5 years old and had no idea what dutchies, koutchies or cannabis were anyway and so I would innocently copy what I heard, imitating the musicians by adopting a kind of fake Jamaican accent as I sang:

I say: Pass the Dutchie on the left-hand side,

Pass the Dutchie on the left-hand side,

It a gonna burn, give me music make me jump and prance,

It a go done, give me the music make me rock in the dance …

Musical Youth followed up their hit single with *Youth of Today*, which reached number thirteen in the UK Singles Chart, and just a few months later their song *Never Gonna Give You Up* climbed to number six in the charts.

But things went downhill from there and despite having some minor successes with their later songs, the band split up and went their separate ways in 1985.

Duran Duran

Nicknamed 'the prettiest boys in rock', Duran Duran were one of the most successful and iconic bands of the 1980s and, according to many women at the time, one of the most beautiful bands as well. The line-up of five sharply dressed, fashionably coiffed young men changed through-out the eighties, but at the time of their first album in 1981 the band comprised front man Simon Le Bon, Nick Rhodes on the keyboard, John Taylor on the bass, Andy Taylor on the guitar and Roger Taylor on the drums. The three Taylors, incidentally, were completely unrelated.

Their first major hit single was *Girls on Film* whose accompanying music video was deliberately provocative, featuring topless women mud wrestling; its intention was to become a sensation that would get people talking about the band. The video was heavily censored and edited in most cases but was shown in its entirety in some of the newer nightclubs that had video screens. The band's highly polished image and daringly provoca-tive music videos made them ideal material for the new music video channel MTV, which helped them gain enormous publicity and turned them into a worldwide success. Throughout the eighties they churned out one hit after another, achieving twelve top-ten hits in the UK in the eighties alone.

The band's next major success was *Hungry Like the Wolf*, released in 1982, which is considered by many to be one of the greatest new wave songs ever recorded; in the same year they reached number two in the charts with *Save a Prayer* and number nine with *Rio*. Their first number one came in 1983 with *Is There Something I Should Know?* This was quickly followed by another number one hit, *The Reflex*, in 1984 and shortly after that was *The Wild Boys*, which made it to number two.

Perhaps their most notable success came in 1985 after John Taylor, the bassist, approached James Bond producer Cubby Broccoli at a party and reportedly asked, somewhat drunkenly, 'When are you going to get someone *decent* to do one of your theme songs?' Surprisingly, instead of being hurled out of the nearest window, the band was offered the opportunity to work with John Barry to create the theme song for the next Bond film, *A View to a Kill*. The eponymously titled song became a worldwide hit, reaching number one in the US and number two in the UK, as well as making the top ten in various other countries.

In total, the boys achieved fourteen top-ten (UK) singles, released thirteen studio albums, sold over 100 million records and broke the hearts of millions of teenage girls.

Michael Jackson

For a while in the 1980s, I became a huge Michael Jackson fan, to the point where I started wearing Michael Jackson pin badges, bought a baseball cap at Blackpool Pleasure Beach that said 'Bad' on it and even asked my mum for some bits of white tape so that I could put them on my fingers, just like my hero. Of course, I looked like a right muppet and my brothers didn't hesitate to tell me so, especially when I combined all this with my usual outfit at the time of a pair of blue checked trousers and a burgundy cardigan. Eventually, I started to become self-conscious in my pink and black 'Bad' baseball cap, so I used a marker pen to alter the first letter so that it now said 'Rad', which was way cooler.

My obsession with Michael Jackson started when I was given my first ever vinyl record, the 1982 Thriller album, which featured a very young-looking Jacko reclining on one elbow in a brilliant white suit and black shirt. I needed a record player to play it on and since my older brother had recently been given one of the new Sony tower hi-fis for his birthday, I inherited his old record player that was mounted in a big wooden cabinet, with ample space below to store my one and only record. Since I only had the one record in my collection, that's all I played, over and over again, and it wasn't long before I knew the lyrics of all the songs: *Wanna Be Startin' Something*, *Baby Be Mine*, *The Girl is Mine*, *Thriller*, *Beat It*, *Billie Jean*, *Human Nature*, *P.Y.T. (Pretty Young Thing)* and *The Lady in my Life*.

Michael Jackson in 1984 attempting to prove that 4 inches of white sock and a single sparkly glove can look cool. *(Public Domain)*

Michael Jackson's musical career is nothing short of astounding, with an unsurpassed track record of thirteen Grammy Awards, twenty-six American Music Awards and dozens of other music awards to make him the most awarded artist in the history of popular music. His album Thriller became the bestselling album of all time with 110 million copies sold and, in total, he is estimated to have sold over 750 million records worldwide.

Not only was Michael Jackson a talented musician and singer, he was also a fantastic dancer and entertainer with a unique style of dancing that included the famous Moonwalk and crotch-grabbing moves that have since been much copied and parodied. I never tried the crotch-grabbing move personally but I do remember shuffling around on the lino floor in the kitchen trying in vain to do the Moonwalk.

There is no shying away from the fact that Michael Jackson led a very mysterious and eccentric personal life that was plagued by controversy and allegations, but I prefer to remember Michael for the music he brought us and the fashion sense he taught me.

Falco

I will always remember Christmas 1985 as the year my brother was given the number one hit single *Rock Me Amadeus* by Falco. Having excitedly opened his gift first thing in the morning, he immediately put the new record on, turned the volume up loud and my brothers and I

danced to it, singing along with the catchy and somewhat repetitive chorus·

Amadeus Amadeus, Amadeus

Amadeus Amadeus, Amadeus

Amadeus Amadeus, oh oh oh Amadeus.

As soon as the song finished, he put it straight back on
so that we could hear it again and this time we worked
on improving our Austrian-accented rap technique as
we tried to copy whatever it was that Falco was saying
in between the choruses. Due to Falco's strong Austrian
accent and rapid-fire rap technique, we struggled to
make out most of the lyrics and so we kept playing the
record over and over again, trying to piece together the
little bits that we could understand. Of course, it wasn't
long before my parents had had enough of the song and
threatened to take the record away if we didn't stop playing it. We never did figure out all the lyrics but realised
that the song was something about the life story of the
classical composer Wolfgang Amadeus Mozart.

Rock Me Amadeus was such a catchy and anthemic song
that it topped the charts in dozens of countries around
the world and became the first single by an Austrian ever
to reach number one in the UK charts. Many people
think of Falco as being a one-hit wonder of the eighties, but in actual fact he made dozens of records and was
hugely popular in his home country where he had eighteen top-ten hits, including five number ones.

Kajagoogoo

In 1982 a relatively unknown avant-garde instrumental group called Art Nouveau placed an advert in *Melody Maker*, the music newspaper:

> Good looking, talented singer/songwriter/frontman, looking for musicians to form what should be a successful band, influences: Japan, Yazoo, Soft Cell … no Des O'Connor fans.

As a result of the advert, the band auditioned and selected Christopher Hamill, who went under the stage name Limahl (an anagram of his surname), and the band changed their name to Kajagoogoo. Shortly afterwards, the newly formed band were spotted by Nick Rhodes, the keyboard player from Duran Duran, who co-produced their first single *Too Shy* with EMI Records.

The single was released in January 1983 and rocketed to the top of the charts where it spent two weeks at number one; it turned the mullet-headed band into a household name virtually overnight. Kajagoogoo had further success with their follow-up singles *Ooh to be Ah* and *Hang on Now*, but barely a year after their first single was released, tensions within the band resulted in Limahl being fired and replaced by Nick Beggs as front man. Another hit single, *Big Apple*, was released in 1984, which reached number eight in the UK charts, but after this the band's popularity declined and their subsequent singles failed to repeat their earlier success.

Freshly fired Limahl decided to use the opportunity to attempt a solo career and sang the theme song to the film *The NeverEnding Story*; it became hugely successful and reached number four in the UK charts. Sadly for him, this was his one and only solo success and poor old Limahl and his famous mullet disappeared into relative obscurity.

Wham!

Having met each other at school in the 1970s, George Michael and Andrew Ridgeley formed a band called Wham! and, while still just teenagers, released their first record *Wham Rap!* in 1982. The record made it into the top ten in the UK charts, while their next record, *Young Guns (Go for It!)*, climbed even higher to achieve a number three position. Over the course of just four years, between 1982 and 1986, the boys released eleven singles, four of which made it to number one in the charts and the remainder making it into the top ten.

Their first number one hit was the unforgettably catchy *Wake Me Up Before You Go-Go*, with a music video that featured Michael and Ridgeley prancing around the stage, dancing like drunken uncles at a wedding party, wearing baggy white t-shirts with the slogan 'Choose LIFE' printed on them. The backing singers, who included the soon-to-be-famous-in-their-own-right Pepsi and Shirlie, all wore white t-shirts with 'GO-GO' written on them.

By this time, the boys had become enormously successful, especially with teenage girls who found the combination of espadrilles, rolled-up jacket sleeves and bouffant hair too heady a look to resist. Their antics of placing shuttlecocks down the front of their shorts during concerts helped them to gain publicity and notoriety, and just one year after their debut, Wham! was already rivalling Duran Duran and Culture Club for the title of Britain's biggest pop act.

Their next song *Freedom* also reached number one in the charts and was closely followed by *Everything She Wants* and *Last Christmas*. In 1985 and 1986, Wham! released three more hits which all made it to number one: *I'm Your Man*, *The Edge of Heaven* and *Where Did Your Heart Go?* before deciding to quit while they were ahead having sold 25 million records together.

A final, emotional farewell concert was held at Wembley Stadium on 28 June 1986 where 73,000 fans witnessed the duo perform for the very last time.

A-ha

In 1982 a trio of Norwegian musicians formed a band called A-ha and left Norway for London to see if they could make a career for themselves in the music business. Morten Harket, the front man, Magne Furuholmen, the keyboard player, and Paul Waaktaar-Savoy, the guitarist, ended up at the studio of musician and producer

John Ratcliff, reputedly enticed by the prospect of his Space Invaders arcade machine; they ultimately ended up hiring Ratcliff and his manager, Terry Slater, to manage their own band.

Two years later, A-ha debuted with their first single, *Take on Me*, which reached number two in the UK charts and number one in the US. The accompanying music video, now considered to be one of the best music videos of all time, helped to boost the popularity of the song and featured a young woman drawn into a fantasy comic-book adventure with lead singer Morten. For some reason, A-ha never really made it big in America and are considered as something of a one-hit wonder there, with *Take on Me* being the only one of their songs to make it into the top ten. But in the UK it was a very different story as their very next single, *The Sun Always Shines on T.V.* from their debut album Hunting High and Low, made it straight to number one.

The next four singles from A-ha all made it into the UK top ten and in 1987 the band reached the peak of their career when they wrote the theme tune for the next Bond film, *The Living Daylights*. One more top-ten track followed with *Stay on These Roads*, but then their popularity began to wane and the chart positions began to drop off. The band continued to perform together right up until 2010 when they announced that they would split.

Spandau Ballet

Some people know Martin Kemp as that bloke who snogged his own mother on *EastEnders*; others know him as the sofa salesman from the SCS television adverts; but I prefer to remember him as the bass guitarist from the New Romantic band Spandau Ballet.

Martin was actually a relatively late addition to the band which had already been started in 1976 by his brother Gary and school friend Steve Norman. By the time Martin joined, the band comprised Gary and Steve on guitars, Tony Hadley as lead singer and John Keeble on the drums.

After signing with Chrysalis Records, the band released their debut single *To Cut a Long Story Short*, which shot to number five in the UK charts in 1980 and catapulted the fashion-conscious quintet to immediate stardom. This success was followed by more hits, such as *The Freeze*, *Musclebound* and the Gold-certified album *Journeys to Glory*, which became one of the defining albums of the early eighties New Romantic movement.

Known as much for their distinctive dress sense as for their iconic music, Tony Hadley once described how his grandfather had refused to travel in the same train carriage as him to show his disapproval of the singer's bizarre outfit. At the time Hadley was wearing ballet slippers, white socks, wraparound Iranian, Cossack-type trousers, tight at the ankles and baggy with a flap up the front, a silk shirt with Greek imprints, make-up and a headband. I sympathise with his grandfather entirely.

In 1983 Spandau Ballet made it to number one with *True* which was closely followed by the anthemic single *Gold*, arguably marking the high point in their musical career. The band continued to churn out singles right through to the end of the eighties, when the band split up and legal proceedings began between band members following a row over royalties. The dust settled eventually and after twenty years apart, the band reunited in 2009 to make a welcome comeback, this time dressing a little more sensibly.

Beastie Boys

The first I heard of the Beastie Boys was in 1986 when my dad read out an article from the newspaper expressing outrage at the sudden spate of thefts of VW badges from the front of cars all over the country. The thieves were stealing the VW badges so that they could wear them around their necks as a fashion accessory, just like their heroes, the Beastie Boys, who had started the trend earlier that year. The situation became so serious that Volkswagen reportedly began offering free replacement badges to all of its customers, and, spotting a marketing opportunity, even provided free badges to Beastie Boys fans. The newspaper article piqued my interest in the band and it wasn't long before I had my hands on the Beastie Boys' debut album Licensed to Ill.

Having started out as a hardcore punk band in the late 1970s, the Beastie Boys didn't actually make the transition to their more familiar hip-hop style until 1984, which meant that their music had a unique sound to it, combining elements of both genres. Consequently, their first album included tracks like *Fight For Your Right*, which was very much a punk track, and *Paul Revere*, which was more of a hip-hop track; and then bridging the two different styles completely were tracks like *No Sleep Till Brooklyn* that incorporated the hard guitars of punk and the rap and drum loops of hip hop.

The debut album was a huge success, particularly in the USA where it reached the number one spot in the charts. In 1989 the boys released their second album Paul's Boutique, which was artistically more mature and less commercially focused. More albums followed in the 1990s and 2000s, and by 2010 the Beastie Boys had sold 40 million albums worldwide.

Prince

Pint-sized, pop prodigy Prince is, without a doubt, one of the most prolific artists in the history of pop music having released hundreds of songs under his own name and under various pseudonyms, as well as writing songs which have been recorded by other artists such as Sinéad O'Connor, The Bangles and Chaka Khan. In addition to his published catalogue of work, he famously has a

Bruce Springsteen performing at a concert in East Germany in 1988, shortly before the fall of the Berlin Wall. *(Courtesy of Bundesarchiv, Uhlemann, Thomas / Wikimedia Commons)*

private vault of unreleased works which is said to include hundreds more songs and over fifty fully produced music videos that have never seen the light of day.

Having released his debut single *Soft and Wet* in 1978, it wasn't until the 1980s that Prince really became popular, beginning with chart successes in America before most of us in the UK had even heard of him. His first foray into the UK charts, with the memorable songs *1999* and *Little Red Corvette*, resulted in a lukewarm response initially, and the two singles only made it into the charts at positions 25 and 54 respectively. It wasn't until several years later, when his popularity and credibility were firmly established, that these songs were re-released and achieved the more rewarding positions of numbers 10 and 2 in the charts.

Prince's first big hit in the UK came in 1984 with *When Doves Cry* from the Purple Rain album, reaching number four in the charts; this was quickly followed by *Purple Rain*, which made it to number eight. The flamboyant and eccentric pop star went on to release hit after hit throughout the eighties, racking up numerous top-ten singles and producing six studio albums, five of which went platinum, with his recording success continuing into the next decade and beyond.

Huey Lewis and the News

If I had to pick just one band that summed up the eighties for me, Huey Lewis and the News would probably be my first choice. There's something so uplifting and fun about their upbeat, pop-rock sound that just seems to sit perfectly with all my favourite memories of my 1980s childhood. However, I'm heavily biased in my opinion because Huey Lewis and the News wrote the soundtrack to my favourite film of all time, *Back to the Future*, and as well as writing the soundtrack, entitled *Back in Time*, their other hit record *The Power of Love* was also featured in the film.

While everyone knows that Ray Parker Jr wrote the theme song to the film *Ghostbusters*, few people realise that the song was actually a direct copy of the Huey Lewis hit *I Want a New Drug*, which sounds laughably similar. In fact, Huey Lewis had originally been asked to write the theme song for *Ghostbusters* but had declined due to his work on *Back to the Future*; his song *I Want a New Drug* was added to the film as a temporary measure during production until Ray Parker Jr concocted his own version of the song. Of course, Huey Lewis wasn't amused at this turn of events and sued Ray Parker Jr for plagiarism, eventually reaching an undisclosed out-of-court settlement.

Shortly after their success with *Back to the Future*, the band went on to release three more hit songs in quick succession: *Stuck with You*, *Hip to be Square* and *Jacob's Ladder*. Two of the songs reached number one in the US charts but achieved more modest results in the UK.

The band's iconic sound became so representative of the 1980s that in the early 1990s its popularity faded and their last major success came in 1991 with *Couple Days Off*.

Guns N' Roses

One of the kids in my class at school became obsessed by Guns N' Roses for a while, in particular the song *Sweet Child o' Mine*, which he would sing over and over again as he stood on his imaginary stage and played his air guitar. Now, it is a great song and many consider it to be one of the best rock songs of all time, but not many people know that it started life as a bit of a joke, when lead guitarist Slash was messing around in a warm-up session and played the now-famous guitar riff while making faces at drummer Steven Adler. Rhythm guitarist Izzy Stradlin asked Slash to play the riff again and a jam session began which inspired lead singer Axl Rose to write some lyrics based on his girlfriend. While the band treated the song flippantly and thought of it as more of a filler track, it became a huge success and made it to number one in the US charts and the UK Rock Chart.

Guns N' Roses formed in 1985 in Los Angeles, California, and their debut studio album Appetite for Destruction was released in 1987, including the tracks *Welcome to the Jungle*, *Paradise City* and, of course, *Sweet Child o' Mine*. No one realised it then, but this album was going to become one of the bestselling albums of all time with sales of around 28 million by the time the album was twenty years old, making it eighteen times platinum certified.

Their second album was released just one year later, entitled G N' R Lies, and was really more of an EP containing just eight tracks; it was the last album to feature the original band line-up before the drummer, Steven Adler, was fired for having become unable to perform adequately due to his cocaine and heroin addiction; he was replaced by Matt Sorum. New member Dizzy Reed also joined around this time as full-time keyboardist and the band went on to release their albums Use Your Illusion I and Use Your Illusion II in the early 1990s. Further albums followed and further changes were made to the line-up until, by the mid-1990s, Axl Rose was the only original band member left.

The Police

My wife's favourite ever song is the 1983 classic from The Police, *Every Breath You Take*, which was the band's fifth number one hit in the UK. Despite superficially sounding like a gentle love song, the lyrics are about a sinister stalker who obsesses over his previous lover, watching 'every breath you take; every move you make'. Apparently Sting, who wrote the song, is disconcerted by the number of people who think the song is an upbeat and positive love song, claiming that some people have even played it at their wedding, oblivious to its dark and ugly significance. I, too, am slightly bewildered that my wife has chosen this song as her favourite, especially since she is perfectly aware of the real meaning behind the lyrics.

The Police originally formed in 1977, the year I was born, and were one of the first new wave bands to become commercially successful. Their musical style contained jazz, punk and even reggae influences which was a unique and highly unusual combination at the time. One of the band's first songs was *Roxanne* which appeared on their debut album Outlandos d'Amour, and it was this song that resulted in the band landing a contract with A&M Records and brought them widespread public recognition. A second album in 1979, Regatta de Blanc, won the Grammy Award for Best Rock Instrumental Performance and included the number one hits *Walking on the Moon* and *Message in a Bottle*.

By the early 1980s the band had embarked on a worldwide tour and produced yet more number one hits, like

Bono from U2 at the Isle of Calf Festival during the War Tour in 1983. Note the mullet haircut. *(Courtesy of Helge Øverås / Wikimedia Commons)*

Don't Stand So Close to Me and *Every Little Thing She Does is Magic*; they also released two more albums, Zenyatta Mondatta and Ghost in the Machine, the latter being an album title which reflected Sting's literary knowledge from his early career as a secondary school English teacher.

Sting became a huge star in his own right and began to spend more and more time developing his interest in acting; but as Sting's fame rose, his relationship with band founder Stewart Copeland deteriorated. In 1983 the band produced its final studio album Synchronicity, before entering a hiatus period and eventually disbanding with each member going on to pursue a solo career.

Black Lace

I still can't believe my mum bought the 7-inch record *Agadoo* by Black Lace; I mean, what was she thinking? And what was everyone else thinking when they bought the record? It is, after all, the worst song of all time by far, and I cannot begin to understand how the song made it to number two in the UK charts or why it stayed in the top seventy-five for thirty weeks.

If we trace the origins of the song right back to the beginning, we can reassuringly blame the French who first recorded it as *Agadou* in 1971. The French, however, deny ownership of the song and claim that it originally came from Morocco, but in the absence of any strong evidence to support this, I'm choosing to blame the French.

It is to my shame that I still remember the lyrics and the dance moves to this day:

Ag-a-doo-doo-doo, push pineapple, shake the tree,

Aga-doo-doo-doo, push pineapple, grind coffee,

To the left, to the right, jump up and down and to the knees,

Come and dance every night, sing with a hula melody.

While Black Lace will always be remembered for *Agadoo*, they did record a number of other songs with moderate success, including the UK's Eurovision Song Contest entry in 1979, *Mary Anne*, a song called *Superman*, which reached number nine in the UK charts in 1982, and *Do the Conga*, which made it to number ten in 1984. They also recorded a string of other lightweight and cheesy songs but most of them never made it into the charts.

Now, before you get *Agadoo* stuck in your head and end up humming it all day, I suggest you cleanse your mind by moving on to something completely different. How about a nice look at the TV and movies of the 1980s in the next chapter?

Four

TV AND MOVIES

When I think about the hundreds of television programmes and movies I fondly remember from the 1980s, I'm really not sure how I managed to find the time to watch them all since I spent the majority of the decade staring vacantly out of a classroom window at school. And when I wasn't at school, I remember spending an awful lot of time playing outside with my friends on our skateboards and BMXs, making camps in the woods or bouncing aimlessly around the garden on an old Space Hopper. And when I wasn't outdoors playing, I would be indoors playing Horace and the Spiders on my ZX Spectrum computer, Top Trumps with my brothers or board games like Buckaroo, Operation and Ker-Plunk. So how did I fit in so much TV viewing as well?

Somehow I managed to watch literally hundreds of television programmes and films in the 1980s, and while

I would dearly love to share my memories of each and every one of them with you, I'm going to have to cherry-pick a few of my favourites since there is simply not enough room in this book to cover them all. At the end of the chapter I've included a full list of the best TV shows and movies of the 1980s which should bring back a few memories.

At the beginning of the 1980s I was a chubby 3-year-old bearing an uncanny resemblance to Ronnie Barker (according to my dad) and consequently, my memories of 1980s television begin with children's programmes before moving on to some more grown-up television.

Button Moon

One of the first new children's television programmes to air in the 1980s was the quirky kitchen-utensil-based puppet show called *Button Moon*. Each episode lasted ten minutes and featured the exploits of Mr Spoon as he left his home on Junk Planet and travelled to Button Moon in his spaceship, which was made of a baked bean tin with a funnel on top. Usually, after landing on Button Moon, which hung in Blanket Sky, Mr Spoon would look through his telescope at someone and have some kind of adventure with his wife Mrs Spoon, his daughter Tina Tea-Spoon and her friend Eggbert. On returning home, the programme would finish with the catchy and slightly melancholy song:

We've been to Button Moon, we've followed Mr Spoon,

Button Moon, Button Moon. We've been to Button Moon,

Button Moon … Be back soon! Button Moon.

The Flumps

An equally peculiar programme around this time was *The Flumps*, an animated story about friendly, hat-wearing fur balls, usually shown just after *Pebble Mill at One*. If you remember anything about *The Flumps*, chances are you will remember the theme tune played by Grandpa Flump on his flumpet (not a trumpet, you understand, a flumpet – there's a world of difference). Poor Grandpa Flump's single pleasure in life was playing the theme song on his flumpet, but he was too noisy for the other Flumps who would shut him up by sticking a carrot in the end of it. Father Flump reminded me of my own dad since he was furry and spent most of his time digging in the garden, and Mother Flump was the stereotypical housewife usually cooking or cleaning around the house. Mother and Father Flump had three children, Perkin, Posie and Pootle. Pootle was the youngest and was always getting things wrong and ending up confused, like the time he thought the moon had fallen into a bucket of water, not realising it was just a reflection.

The Moomins

While we were still trying to make sense of *The Flumps*, a strange family of Fuzzy Felt, hippo-like creatures with huge round snouts called *The Moomins* appeared on our television screens to addle our young minds further. *The Moomins* was the eccentric creation of Finnish author Tove Jansson and they were a family of trolls who lived in a house in Moominvalley, deep in the forests of Finland. Moominmama and Moominpappa had a Moomin son called Moomintroll and during their many adventures they would encounter other characters such as Moomintroll's best friend, the Snork Maiden; Snufkin, the pipe-smoking old man; Sorry-oo, the mournful dog; Little My and The Hemulen. These and the many other strange denizens of Moominvalley had a number of adventures together, as well as assisting each other against the dangers posed by various villainous creatures, including the terrifying Groke, the Hattifatteners who lived on electricity, and the bad-tempered Sand Lion.

Fraggle Rock

Fraggle Rock was a live-action puppet show created by Jim Henson. It featured Muppet-like characters called fraggles that lived in a network of caves within Fraggle Rock which was located underneath a lighthouse. The main characters were Gobo, the leader; Mokey, a far-out hippie type; Red, an exuberant and athletic fraggle; Wembley, the indecisive one (or was he?); and Boober, a depressed and worried fraggle that enjoyed washing socks. It was certainly strange that Boober enjoyed washing socks, but it was stranger still when you realised that none of the fraggles actually wore socks.

These peaceful and playful furry critters would spend most of their time stealing radishes from the garden of the giant Gorgs and avoiding being caught by them. Sometimes, while in the Gorgs' garden, the fraggles would talk to Marjory the Trash Heap, a kind of wise oracle made out of garden waste who would give the fraggles advice. At other times the fraggles would eat the elaborate structures constructed by the small, green creatures called the Doozers. The only one from the real world who knew about the existence of the fraggles was the lighthouse keeper's dog Sprocket, who would spot Gobo when he came out to collect postcards from Uncle Travelling Matt, the globe-trotting fraggle.

Jim'll Fix It

A shell-suited and blinged-up Jimmy Savile used to host this Saturday teatime show which featured members of the public writing in to ask for help achieving their dreams. The handwritten letter would be shown on the screen as a voice narrated: 'Dear Jim'll, please could you fix it for the 2nd Sutton St Mary's Cub Scouts to have a meal in an unusual place?' You may well remember this episode which resulted in a group of the aforementioned Cub Scouts being sent to Blackpool Pleasure Beach with a packed lunch to eat as they rode the Revolution roller-coaster, with hilarious consequences. Some of the other more memorable requests included one young viewer briefly becoming the third drummer for Adam and the Ants and a young girl 'accidentally' dropping a seemingly valuable vase on an episode of the *Antiques Roadshow* in order to enjoy the audience reaction.

After having their wishes granted they were presented with a 'Jim fixed it for me' medal which Jim would produce from a secret compartment inside his magic chair.

Treasure Hunt

Treasure Hunt was the TV show that launched jumpsuit-clad Anneka Rice into the public consciousness. The bubbly blonde would fly from location to location in a helicopter, making small talk with the camera while the studio team used maps and reference books to solve cryptic clues that would lead to the location of the treasure. In the studio, presenter Kenneth Kendal and weathergirl Wincey Willis tried to support the guest treasure hunters as best they could and kept the show on track and on time. Once the studio team had identified the correct location, the helicopter would land and Anneka Rice would bounce out and run off at great speed to find the next clue. Since the clues often made no sense to anyone other than the locals, Anneka would inevitably end up grabbing confused passers-by and asking for their assistance. Legendary cameraman Graham had to keep up with Anneka, running just as fast as her with a heavy shoulder-mounted camera, and he became an unexpected star of the show as he often appeared in front of the camera lens to wipe away rain and sea spray. Much of poor Graham's footage comprised shots of Anneka Rice's jumpsuited backside as he attempted to follow her from location to location.

The Krypton Factor

Gordon Burns famously hosted this mental and physical challenge show which involved putting contestants through a series of gruelling logic tests and assault courses. First up was the Mental Agility Round in which the contestants had to answer mind-bending questions; this was followed by the Response Round, which involved trying to land an aeroplane in a flight simulator. The Observation Round was always my favourite and involved watching a video clip and then answering questions like 'What was the colour of the glove on the table?'

Physical Ability was the round that saw the contestants each take to an army assault course, during which they would brave rope swings, water jumps and endure a zip-wire slide into water. After this came the Intelligence

Round, in which various odd-shaped pieces would have to be put together to fit a rectangular grid or other shape; some of these puzzles were so fiendish that they took 15–20 minutes to complete. On one occasion, the contestants' tables were placed too close together which meant that they accidentally picked up pieces from each others' tables, making it impossible to complete the puzzle. Nearly an hour went by as they tried in vain to solve the puzzle before someone finally realised what had happened.

The last round, General Knowledge, was a series of quick-fire questions which concluded the show and led to Gordon Burns adding up the scores and announcing the name of the winning contestant. The well-known theme tune to *The Krypton Factor* was played by the Art of Noise.

Blockbusters

'Can I have a "P" please, Bob?' Oh, how funny we used to think that was! *Blockbusters* was a game show presented by Bob Holness in which contestants had to answer trivia questions in order to complete a path across or down the game board which was made of hexagons. Answering questions correctly didn't guarantee you success, though, since there was a fiendish strategy involved in crossing the playing board and preventing your opponent from getting to the other side first.

Sometimes the pressure would be too much for the nervous contestants, who would blurt out the most ridiculous and inappropriate answers, such as, 'What "O" is the generic word for any living animal or plant, including bacteria and viruses?' The contestant confidently replied, 'Orgasm', before realising the enormity of his momentary lapse.

Blockbusters was so popular it spawned an array of associated merchandise, including the Waddington's board game which I thoroughly enjoyed playing with my family – 'Can I have a "P" please, mum?' Snigger.

Open All Hours

'G-G-Granville! F-fetch yer cloth!' This comedy series was penned by Roy Clarke, who also wrote *Last of the Summer Wine* and *Keeping Up Appearances*, and featured Ronnie Barker as Albert Arkwright, the miserly shopkeeper with a stutter, and his nephew Granville, played by a young David Jason. Poor Granville was a wistful and philosophical errand boy whose sole aim in life was to have a meaningful relationship with a woman, but his attempts were usually frustrated by his mean-spirited and selfish uncle who made him work long hours and gave him little freedom. Much of Arkwright's time was spent trying to persuade his voluptuous long-term fiancée, Nurse Gladys Emmanuel, to marry him. Twenty-six episodes were made in all with the last instalment in 1985.

Lovejoy

If I ever hear anyone use the phrase 'lovable rogue', I immediately conjure up a mental image of Lovejoy dressed in a black leather jacket, white t-shirt, cowboy boots and sporting a horrific mullet/perm combo haircut.

Ian McShane as lovable rogue and dodgy antique dealer Lovejoy. If you could see the rest of him in the picture, he would undoubtedly be wearing cowboy boots and an uncomfortably tight pair of stonewashed denim jeans. *(BBC)*

Ian McShane starred as the 'lovable rogue' Lovejoy who was a dodgy antiques dealer with a reputation for being a 'divvie', meaning one who has an almost magical ability to discern valuable items and to spot forgeries. Lovejoy embarked on roguish adventures which often involved burglary and forgery – but normally only in the course of justice, revenge or love. Lovejoy was sometimes assisted in his exploits by his alcoholic colleague Tinker and dim-witted friend Eric, and in some cases he was helped by his love interest, Lady Jane Felsham, or in later episodes by Charlotte Cavendish.

Lovejoy's unorthodox activities landed him in trouble on a number of occasions and he was even sent to prison at one point, although strangely it wasn't for the crimes against fashion that he had committed.

Spitting Image

The anarchic and satirical puppet show *Spitting Image* first aired in 1984 on ITV and featured a host of well-known politicians and celebrities caricatured as rubber puppets. Much of the show focused on Margaret Thatcher, Ronald Reagan and the British royal family, with Mrs T portrayed as a bullying macho tyrant who dressed as a man and used the male urinals. John Major's puppet was always dressed in different shades of grey, skin included; Douglas Hurd had a Dalek-style voice with a Mr Whippy haircut; and the Queen Mum was usually shown holding a bottle of gin, a copy of the *Racing Post* and talking with a Beryl Reid voice.

In addition to the satirical sketches, *Spitting Image* produced a number of musical parodies, the most notable being *The Chicken Song*, which surprisingly made it to number one in the charts for three weeks and was a parody of the Black Lace song *Agadoo*. I can still remember most of the words to *The Chicken Song* thanks to its incessant repetition on the radio, in the school playground and at home on the record player:

Hold a chicken in the air,
Stick a deckchair up your nose,
Buy a jumbo jet,
And then bury all your clothes,
Paint your left knee green,
Then extract your wisdom teeth,
Form a string quartet,
And pretend your name is Keith.

Having been one of the numerous people who bought the vinyl record of *The Chicken Song*, I can tell you that the B side was an even more amusing, though highly offensive, song entitled *I've Never Met a Nice South African*, which was a savage indictment of the apartheid-ridden country.

The A-Team

In 1972, a crack commando unit was sent to prison by a military court for a crime they didn't commit. These men promptly escaped from a maximum security stockade to the Los Angeles underground. Today, still wanted by the government, they survive as soldiers of fortune. If you have a problem, if no one else can help, and if you can find them, maybe you can hire … The A-Team.

I certainly could have used the help of the A-Team on a number of occasions but I could never find them, despite their distinctive black GMC Vandura van.

The A-Team is undoubtedly one of the most iconic television shows of the 1980s, telling the story of four Vietnam veterans who escape from prison after being wrongly accused of robbing a bank. The team was led by John Hannibal Smith, played by George Peppard, and included Templeton 'Face' Peck, the ladies' man, 'Howling Mad' Murdoch, the insane team pilot, and strongman B.A. Baracus, played by Mr T. Every episode featured gun fights, explosions and lots of exciting and violent action, but somehow people rarely got hurt, even the bad guys. The A-Team would often get captured by their enemies and end up fashioning an improbable weapon from whatever was lying around to help them make their escape, and Face would inevitably become attracted to whoever the female lead was in that episode.

The show became so popular that by the fourth season guest stars, including Boy George and Hulk Hogan, appeared as themselves and the numerous catchphrases used by the A-Team made their way into popular culture, such as 'I love it when a plan comes together' and 'I ain't gettin' on no plane!'

John Craven's Newsround

I remember feeling very grown up watching *John Craven's Newsround* since the news was something that adults watched. The ten-minute news programme presented by John Craven was aimed at 6- to 12-year-olds and comprised a brief, palatable summary of current affairs and world news. Most memorably, *Newsround* was the first programme in Britain to report the loss of the Space Shuttle Challenger, with dramatic images of the disintegrating spacecraft shown during the opening titles.

The Two Ronnies

Ronnie Corbett and Ronnie Barker were, without a doubt, one of the funniest and most popular comedy double acts of all time, following closely on the heels of Morecambe and Wise. Their BBC1 sketch show, *The Two Ronnies*, attracted viewing figures of 20 million at its peak and ran for sixteen years over twelve series; it attracted numerous guest stars including Elkie Brooks, Elton John, Elaine Paige and Phil Collins, among others. The opening credits would feature the familiar theme music and a picture of two pairs of spectacles, representing those of Ronnie B and Ronnie C, before cutting to the 'newsdesk' where the Ronnies would take it in turns to read spoof news stories.

Perhaps the most famous *Two Ronnies* sketch is 'Four Candles' written by Ronnie Barker, who had a talent for wordplay humour. Ronnie Barker plays a customer in a hardware store with a shopping list; he asks for what sounds like 'four candles' but, after being given the candles, corrects the shopkeeper by explaining that he meant 'fork 'andles, for garden forks'. The list continues with numerous other confusing items before the shopkeeper gives up when he is asked for 'billhooks', at which point you need to use your imagination to understand how that could be humorously mispronounced.

Both Ronnies seemed to enjoy dressing up in outlandish costumes for their characters, particularly Ronnie B, who spent a lot of time wearing ladies' clothes, and the sketches sometimes turned into elaborate musical productions. Ronnie Corbett would always have a monologue at some point in the show when he would sit in a chair facing the camera attempting to tell a simple joke but continually getting sidetracked by other humorous reflections. The show closed with the 'newsdesk' again and a rapid fire of spoof news, before the Ronnies signed off with their catchphrase:

Corbett: So it's 'Goodnight' from me.

Barker: And it's 'Goodnight' from him.

Both: Goodnight!

Television Adverts

Do you remember George the Hofmeister bear? He was the football-playing, beer-drinking, laddish equivalent of the Honey Monster. Well, my parents picked up a t-shirt at a jumble sale for me with a message on the front that read, 'I've got a bear behind', and on the back was a picture of George the Hofmeister bear, grinning, winking and giving a thumbs-up. I was 9. What were they thinking?

George the bear was just one of many characters created for television advertising purposes, and the next one that springs to mind is British Telecom's Buzby, the fat yellow bird voiced by Bernard Cribbins who told us to 'Make someone happy with a phone call'. Smash had the aliens, Sugar Puffs had the Honey Monster and Frosties had Tony the Tiger, but Hamlet cigars had Gregor Fisher with a dodgy comb-over. In each instalment of the Hamlet cigar ads, some calamity would befall the lead character who would immediately light up a cigar as consolation while the 'Hamlet song' was played on the piano. Gregor Fisher, better known as 'that bloke who played Rab C. Nesbitt', featured in one of the best-remembered Hamlet ads, taking the role of an overweight and unattractive middle-aged man with a Bobby Charlton comb-over. He takes a seat in a photo booth and arranges his wisp of hair to perfection, then he sits back and waits for the photo. Nothing happens so he leans forward to look at the machine; at that exact moment the flash goes off taking a picture of the top of his head. He tries again and the same thing happens, and on the third and final attempt the chair suddenly drops just before the photograph is taken. Cue the Hamlet music and a puff of smoke from a smiling Rab C. Nesbitt.

Perhaps my favourite advert of the 1980s is the famous Heineken 'water in Majorca' ad. A well-spoken young Sloane Ranger visits the School of Street Credibility, where Bryan Pringle plays a frustrated voice coach trying to teach his pupil how to speak in a cockney accent. After several posh-sounding attempts at reciting 'The water in Majorca don't taste like what it ought to', an assistant brings the young lady a can of Heineken, and says, 'Get yer larfin' gear around that.' After a sip of the beer the lady tries again and this time recites the words in a strong cockney accent, which gets even stronger after a second mouthful of the drink. The advert finishes with the slogan 'Heineken refreshes the parts wot other beers cannot reach'.

Can you believe it's time to leave the TV section already and move on to some of the movies of the eighties? Hey, there's no need to yell at me, I know that I've barely scratched the surface of the TV shows but there really was so much good stuff in the eighties that it's impossible to fit even a fraction of it in here. If you want to see a full list of my favourite TV shows from the eighties, skip straight to the end of the chapter. OK, ready to move on? Lights, cameras, action …

Back to the Future

Michael J. Fox stars as teenager Marty McFly whose eccentric friend Doc Emmett Brown (Christopher Lloyd) invents a time machine which he installs in a DeLorean car. The famous flux capacitor is at the heart of the machine and is activated when the car reaches 88mph, sending the occupant through time to the date entered in the console. In this case, Marty is sent back to 1955 where he visits his home town of Hill Valley and meets his parents as teenagers.

Marty's young mother Lorraine rather disturbingly develops a crush on him, which leads to the possibility that she won't fall in love with his father at the Enchantment Under the Sea dance where they are supposed to share their first kiss. Marty tries to matchmake his mother and father George while also trying to persuade the young Doc Brown to help him get back to the future that he belongs to: 1985.

Marty hatches a plan to make George look like a hero to Lorraine by staging a confrontation in the school parking lot. However, the plan goes awry when Biff Tannen, the school bully, makes an unexpected appearance and tries to force himself on Lorraine in the car. Marty's dad George, not knowing it is Biff in the car and thinking it is part of the plan, confronts the assailant and, after some abuse, decides that he has finally put up with enough from the bully and punches him out cold.

Back to the Future (1985), starring Michael J. Fox and Christopher Lloyd. *(Universal)*

George's assertiveness makes Lorraine fall in love with him and secures a happy future for the McFly family. Doc Brown, in the meantime, figures out an elaborate scheme to harness the energy from a lightning bolt to send the DeLorean and Marty back to 1985.

Not only does the film have the perfect mix of comedy, action, drama and romance, but there are some great skateboarding sequences, an unforgettable sound-track and some memorable acting from Michael J. Fox. Two sequels were made a few years later where Marty travels into the grim future of 2015 and then back to an 1885 cowboy town.

Police Academy

Steve Guttenberg stars as Cadet Carey Mahoney in this classic comedy set in a police training academy. Mahoney is a repeat offender sentenced to join the academy as punishment under a new scheme proposed by the mayor, whereby the police department must accept all willing recruits. Mahoney is joined by an assortment of misfits, including gun-loving Eugene Tackleberry, superhuman ex-florist Hightower and sound-effects specialist Larvell Jones, among others.

Cadet Mahoney tries his best to get himself expelled from the academy through a series of pranks aimed at Captain Harris, his superior, but under the terms of his punishment he is compelled to stay and serve his time.

As it happens, he ends up enjoying his time at the police academy thanks, in part, to the presence of sexy female cadet Karen Thompson, played by Kim Cattrall.

Of all the characters in the seven *Police Academy* films that were made, my favourite character was that of Tackleberry whose profound love of firearms often led to his naive overuse of weaponry to solve simple problems; for example, he helps an old lady who has lost her coin in a payphone by shooting it open, holding out a handful of coins and asking, 'Can you identify your quarter, ma'am?'

Ghostbusters

Bill Murray (Venkman), Dan Ackroyd (Stantz) and Harold Ramis (Spengler) star in this 1984 supernatural comedy about three parapsychologists who set up a business in New York to catch ghosts in a similar manner to pest controllers. After catching and containing their first ghosts, the team become celebrities and are hired to clean up the city from the increasing number of ghosts, eventually hiring a fourth Ghostbuster, Winston (Ernie Hudson), to assist them. Everything seems to be going pretty well until the Ghostbusters are called to investigate a demonic spirit called Zuul which appears to be living in Sigourney Weaver's fridge. As it turns out, the fridge is a portal to a spiritual realm where the demigod Gozer the Gozerian lives, who is planning to visit New York and bring about the end of the world.

As the Ghostbusters plan their strategy for preventing the appearance of Gozer, a visit from the US Environmental Protection Agency, who suspect the use of dangerous chemicals, leads to the Ghostbusters' facilities being shut down. The ghost containment machine is deactivated which releases all the ghosts back into the city, causing mayhem, and the Ghostbusters are arrested for operating an unlicensed nuclear device in their basement.

With the Ghostbusters in captivity, Gozer appears, and the mayor has to release the men when he realises they are the only people who can prevent the impending disaster. Gozer arrives in the form of a woman and declares that the 'destructor' will follow and he will take the form of whatever the Ghostbusters first think of. Unable to keep his mind blank, Stantz tries to think of 'something that could never, ever possibly destroy us', whereupon the 'destructor' emerges as a giant Stay Puft Marshmallow Man. The giant Marshmallow Man starts to destroy the city but is eventually stopped by the Ghostbusters, who dangerously cross their energy streams in order to blow him up.

After watching this film, my friends and I decided to become Ghostbusters ourselves and spent many playtimes on the hunt for ghosts in the school playground. My best friend at the time tried to convince me that he had actually seen a ghost at home and had even collected some of its ectoplasm. The next day he brought in a little bottle with some green slime in it that looked convincing but smelled of shampoo.

Big

In the 1988 romantic comedy *Big*, Tom Hanks plays a young boy, Josh Baskin, who is magically aged to adulthood overnight. After being refused entry to a fairground ride for being too short, 13-year-old Josh tries his luck with the Zoltar Speaks fortune-telling machine and makes a wish to be big. The machine magically responds, despite not being plugged in, and Josh backs away.

The next morning, Josh awakes to discover, to his horror, that he has become an adult overnight and is now a 30-year-old man, terrifying his mother who thinks that he is a crazed kidnapper that has abducted her son. Josh flees and with the help of his best friend Billy gets himself a data entry job at the MacMillan Toy Company. Josh's childlike enthusiasm for the toys they produce results in his promotion to a dream job which involves testing toys all day long and getting paid for it. It's not long before Josh attracts the attention of the beautiful 27-year-old Susan and a romance begins to develop. As Josh becomes increasingly involved in his adult lifestyle, he begins to forget his friend Billy and tensions mount between the pair. Eventually, Josh concludes that he would prefer to revert to his childhood life and returns to the Zoltar machine where he makes a wish to be a child once more.

There are plenty of gags to be had in this movie and many memorable scenes, including Hanks playing *Chopsticks* on the giant foot-operated keyboard in the toy store, and singing the secret 'shimmy shimmy cocoa pop' song to his best friend to convince him that he really is who he says he is. The very same year *Big* was released, the film *Vice Versa* also appeared in cinemas, bearing an uncanny similarity, with a young boy and his father magically trading bodies so that the child becomes an adult and 'vice versa'.

Dirty Dancing

Everybody knows the catchphrase 'Nobody puts Baby in a corner' and everyone remembers that dance move where Baby jumps up above Patrick Swayze's head, arms outstretched. In fact, you still hear the catchphrase in use today and you still see people attempting the dance move in countless wedding dance videos on the internet. Released in 1987, *Dirty Dancing* was the last of the big eighties' dance movies, following on from the likes of *Fame* (1980), *Flashdance* (1983) and *Footloose* (1984). Patrick Swayze played resident dance instructor Johnny Castle at the Kellerman's holiday resort in the Catskill Mountains and Jennifer Grey played Frances 'Baby' Houseman, the 17-year-old New Yorker who falls in love with Johnny while vacationing with her well-to-do family. The film is essentially a coming-of-age drama, with Baby secretly dating the working-class dancer while learning to dance herself so that she can be a substitute dancer at the annual performance. Despite opposition from her parents, she continues her relationship and ultimately performs an impromptu final dance of the season with Johnny in front of her parents, climaxing with the famous dance lift move to the music of *(I've Had) The Time of My Life*. To this day, every time I hear that song, I grab the nearest woman I can find and lift them up over my head.

Ferris Bueller's Day Off

If you had to choose the best film of the 1980s, chances are you would pick this one. Matthew Broderick plays the cooler-than-cool Ferris Bueller, the popular kid you always wanted to be, who fakes illness to take a day off school with his highly strung friend Cameron and his beautiful girlfriend Sloane.

Ferris and his friends enjoy the illicit freedom from school, enhanced by 'borrowing' Cameron's father's Ferrari 250 GT California for the day. But not everyone is convinced by Ferris's fake illness; his jealous sister Jeanie uncovers the deception and sets out to blow his cover, while the evil school dean of students, Edward Rooney, also believes Ferris to be a truant and attempts to catch him out. Everyone else thinks Ferris is unwell and since he is so popular, he gains a huge amount of sympathy and attention, much to the annoyance of his sister.

Mr Rooney visits Ferris at home but is greeted by a recorded message when pushing the intercom button.

Matthew Broderick starred as Ferris Bueller in this 1986 classic movie. *(Paramount)*

Smelling a rat, Rooney tries to break into the house, losing a shoe in the mud in the process, and is met by Jeanie who high-kicks him in the face and runs upstairs to call the police. Later at the police station, Jeanie ends up making out with Charlie Sheen who plays an arrested drug addict.

Meanwhile, Ferris, Cameron and Sloane have a whale of a time at the Von Steuben Day parade in town, with Ferris dancing atop one of the floats and lip-syncing to *Twist and Shout*. On returning to the Ferrari they discover it has been used by the parking attendants and has hundreds of miles on the odometer, sending Cameron into a panic attack. After unsuccessfully trying to take the miles off the clock by jacking up the car and running it in reverse, Cameron realises that he is going to have to face up to his father about what he has done. As he comes to terms with this situation, he leans on the Ferrari, knocking it off the axle stands and sending it reversing at high speed out of the garage, whereby it crashes into the ravine beyond.

After an eventful day of high jinx, Ferris heads home, just ahead of his parents as they return from work, to pretend he has spent the whole day in bed. The hateful Mr Rooney is attacked by the Buellers' dog and ends up having to hitch a ride home, dishevelled, shoeless and sore.

Next time you watch the film (and you will watch it again, I'm sure) check out the license plates of the various vehicles used and you'll spot abbreviated references to other films made by the same director, John

Hughes. Katie's = VCTN (*National Lampoon's Vacation*); Jeanie's = TBC (*The Breakfast Club*); Tom's = MMOM (*Mr Mom*); Rooney's = 4FBDO (*Ferris Bueller's Day Off*). The exception is Cameron's dad's Ferrari (seen when Ferris first pulls out of the garage), the license plate of which reads NRVOUS.

National Lampoon's Christmas Vacation

They still show this film every Christmas, and I still watch it every Christmas. I know all the jokes and anticipate every event, but it still makes me laugh. Chevy Chase plays Clark, the highly strung father of the Griswold family nearing nervous breakdown due to his usual over-enthusiasm about making Christmas perfect. His long-suffering but supportive wife Ellen accompanies him on a trip into the forest to find the perfect Christmas tree; they return with a vastly oversized tree that barely fits in the house and is home to a well-hidden squirrel that wreaks havoc later in the film. Clark decorates his house with 25,000 Christmas lights, along with an assortment of animated seasonal characters, but struggles to get the power on much to the disappointment of his assembled family. After fixing the lighting problem he eventually switches on, causing a power drain at the nuclear power plant and ends up blinding the neighbours. Things seem to be going well until Clark's cousin Eddie and his family turn up unexpectedly and all the Christmas plans go awry. After Clark discovers that he will not be getting the Christmas bonus that he was expecting, his helpful cousin kidnaps the boss and brings him back to the house to 'persuade' him to change his mind. As you would expect, the movie concludes happily with Clark getting his bonus and everybody enjoying a family Christmas together, despite the mayhem.

Top Gun

In a strange and somewhat disturbing parallel universe somewhere, there is another version of the 1986 film *Top Gun*, the only difference being that when Maverick steps out of his fighter aircraft and takes off his pilot's helmet, you see the goofy smile of Jim Carrey rather than the good looks of Tom Cruise. How weird would that be? But bizarre as that may seem, Jim Carrey really was considered for the lead role, along with John Travolta and Robert Downey Junior. In fact, Tom Cruise wasn't even the first choice since the producers had already asked Patrick Swayze, Emilio Estevez, Nicolas Cage, John Cusack, Matthew Broderick, Sean Penn, Michael J. Fox and Tom Hanks, who all turned down the role. Thankfully, Tom Cruise accepted the part and became the star of one of the most successful films of all time which has grossed over $344 million worldwide to date.

Cruise plays the hotshot fighter pilot Maverick, who rises to the top of the class at the Top Gun Naval

Flying School and vies for superiority with his nemesis, Iceman, played by Val Kilmer. A sexy naval instructor (Kelly McGillis) arrives on the scene and falls in love with Maverick, adding a much-needed romantic dimension to the otherwise tedious plot of the film. After being involved in a fatal flying accident, which kills his best friend Goose, Maverick loses his nerve and nearly leaves the air force altogether; but he manages to keep it together in order to fight off some enemy MiG fighters. That's about it really. Not the most engaging storyline in the world but this is more than made up for by the fantastic soundtrack and awesome aviation action sequences.

One of my school friends became so enthralled by the film that at the age of 10 he decided that he would one day become a fighter pilot himself. And some years later, that's exactly what he did. In fact, after the release of the film, the US Navy revealed that the number of young men enlisting to be navy aviators went up by 500 per cent!

The NeverEnding Story

Our hero in this film is a young boy called Bastian who escapes bullying by reading a magical book that transports him to the world of Fantasia; here, the Empress pleads with him to save them from a terrible force that threatens the whole world called The Nothing. Bastian is assisted by Atreyu, a young warrior, and a luckdragon named Falkor (who looked a lot like my parents' Pekingese dog called Ming). The terrible Nothing spreads through the world, destroying it piece by piece as Bastian travels across the mystical land encountering numerous bizarre creatures and challenges along the way. We discover that Fantasia represents humanity's hopes and dreams and that The Nothing represents apathy, cynicism and the denial of childish dreams. Ultimately, Bastian makes it to the Empress' ivory tower, but by the time he arrives the whole of Fantasia has been destroyed. After concluding his mission by giving the Empress her new name of Moonchild, the Empress then tells Bastian that he can restore all of Fantasia just by wishing it and using his imagination. The film ends with Bastian flying on the back of Falkor over the restored land of Fantasia, before making a sneaky detour to terrify the bullies back home in the real world.

War Games

Back in 1983 when the film *War Games* was released, many British homes had recently purchased a BBC Micro, ZX Spectrum or Commodore 64 computer and were just beginning to understand the power and potential of home computers. What they didn't realise, though, was that their home computer had the potential to inadvertently start a Thermonuclear War. In this cold war suspense film, Matthew Broderick plays young computer hacker David Lightman who accidentally accesses a US military supercomputer programmed to predict possible outcomes of a nuclear war.

Lightman begins by trying to impress his friend Jennifer (Ally Sheedy), showing her how he can hack into the school computer and change her failing grades. As he demonstrates his hacking skills, he comes across an unidentified computer which he believes contains various games he can play, including Theaterwide Biotoxic, Chemical Warfare and Global Thermonuclear War. What he doesn't realise is that this is actually a back door into a military computer that controls America's automated missile silos using a kind of artificial intelligence which learns from the outcomes of the various hypothetical 'war game' scenarios it runs. As they begin a 'game of Global Thermonuclear War', the North American Aerospace Defense Command (NORAD) control centre believes that actual Soviet missiles have been launched and are heading for strategic targets in the US, although it soon becomes evident that this has not actually occurred. Although no Soviet missiles have been launched, the NORAD supercomputer thinks that missiles have been fired and automatically prepares retaliatory action that will lead to World War III.

Lightman discovers what has happened from a news broadcast and although he tries to cover his tracks, he is quickly arrested by the FBI and taken in for questioning. Lightman realises the severity of the situation and escapes, tracking down the original programmer of the NORAD supercomputer to ask for his help in preventing a nuclear holocaust.

Disaster is averted at the very last moment after Lightman directs the computer to play tic-tac-toe against itself, resulting in a long string of draws and thereby teaching the computer the concept of futility. Just before launching the nuclear missiles, the computer runs through all the possible outcomes of the thermonuclear war and realises they all result in stalemates, at which point the computer decides that nuclear warfare is 'a strange game' and offers to play a nice game of chess instead.

E.T. The Extra-Terrestrial

This is without doubt one of the greatest science fiction films of the 1980s, telling the story of a lonely boy called Elliott who discovers an alien living in the woods near his home. Some visiting alien botanists had been exploring the woods together but were scared off by US government agents; in their haste to escape, they accidentally leave behind E.T. the extra-terrestrial. Fortunately, this alien is not one of the laser-wielding, blood-sucking varieties and instead prefers watching movies and getting drunk while his new friend Elliott is at school. Everything goes well for a while, although E.T. seems to be missing home and attempts to communicate with his home planet using a makeshift transmitter cobbled together from odds and ends wired to a Speak and Spell toy. E.T. demonstrates some remarkable talents, including reanimating a dead flower, healing an injured finger and using a psychic connection to transfer his emotions to Elliott.

Things start to get a bit edgy when E.T. falls ill; due to his psychic connection, Elliott also gets sick and it becomes evident that the pair are dying. At this point, government agents raid the house and quarantine both Elliott and E.T. in a rather intense and frightening scene which terrified me as a child. It appears as though E.T. dies and Elliott begins to recover, but when Elliott is left alone with E.T., he reanimates and reveals that his alien buddies are coming back to retrieve him. Now all they have to do is escape from the government agents and get to the alien landing site as quickly as possible, giving rise to a heart-pounding BMX bike chase sequence with E.T. in a basket on the front of Elliott's bike. Trapped in a dead-end, E.T. conveniently demonstrates another of his skills by levitating the bicycle in the air leading to the often-parodied silhouetted-bicycle-in-front-of-the-full-moon shot.

Of course, E.T. makes it back to his spaceship just in time and disappears back off to his home planet, leaving Elliot and his sister Gertie (Drew Barrymore) staring up at a rainbow in the sky. At the time, *E.T.* was the second most financially successful film ever, after *Star Wars*, taking a whopping $792,910,554 at box offices worldwide, as well as generating vast revenues from related merchandise.

While I would dearly love to continue reminiscing about all the other films I enjoyed in the 1980s, I'm going to have to wrap it up because there's simply not enough space in this book to cover them all. Instead, I'll leave you with a nostalgic list of some of my personal favourite films and TV shows of the eighties. Please note that I have been careful to only include films that were actually released in the 1980s, but you may notice that some of the TV shows span more than one decade. Of course, a lot of what we watched on television in the eighties was a continuation of existing TV shows that had started back in the seventies.

TV Shows of the 1980s

A Bit of a Do
Airwolf
Alexei Sayle's Stuff
All Creatures Great & Small
'Allo 'Allo
Are You Being Served?
Auf Weidersehen, Pet
Bananaman
Battle of the Planets
Baywatch
Beadle's About
Bergerac
Blankety Blank
Blind Date
Blue Peter
Blue Thunder

Brookside
Brush Strokes
Button Moon
Byker Grove
Cagney & Lacey
Cannon & Ball
Catch Phrase
Challenge Anneka
Charlie's Angels
Cheggers Plays Pop
Chip 'n Dale Rescue Rangers
Chish 'n Fips
Chockablock
Citizen Smith
Clive James on Television
Colin's Sandwich
Columbo
Come Dancing
Coronation Street
Countdown
Crackerjack
Crimewatch UK
Crossroads
Dallas
Danger Mouse
Dear John
Degrassi Junior High
Des O'Connor Now
Diff'rent Strokes

Dogtanian & the Three Muskehounds
Doogie Howser, M.D.
Dr Who
Duck Tales
Dynasty
EastEnders
Emmerdale Farm
Eurovision Song Contest
Family Fortunes
Finger Mouse
Fraggle Rock
French and Saunders
Friday Night Live
Give Us a Clue
Grandstand
Grange Hill
Hale & Pace
Hardcastle & McCormick
Hawaii Five-O
He-Man & the Masters of the Universe
Henry's Cat
Hi-de-Hi!
Howards' Way
Inspector Gadget
It Ain't Half Hot Mum
It's a Knockout
Jackanory
James the Cat
Jamie and the Magic Torch

Jem and The Holograms
Jimbo and the Jet-Set
Jim'll Fix It
John Craven's Newsround
Jonny Briggs
Jossy's Giants
Juliet Bravo
The Kenny Everett Television Show
The Kids of Degrassi Street
King Rollo
Knightmare
Knight Rider
Knots Landing
LA Law
Last of the Summer Wine
Let's Pretend
Little House on the Prairie
London's Burning
Lovejoy
M.A.S.H.
M.A.S.K.
Magnum P.I.
Manimal
Married with Children
Mastermind
Match of the Day
Max Headroom
Mike Yarwood in Persons
Minder

Miss World
Monkey
Monty Python's Flying Circus
Mork & Mindy
Mr & Mrs
Multi-Coloured Swap Shop
Munch Bunch
Murder She Wrote
My Little Pony 'n Friends
My Two Dads
Naked Video
Neighbours
Noggin the Nog
Not the Nine O'Clock News
Only Fools and Horses
Open All Hours
Opportunity Knocks
Pebble Mill at One
Pigeon Street
Play Away
Play School
Play Your Cards Right
Points of View
Police Squad!
Popeye
Porterhouse Blue
Prisoner (Cell Block H)
Puddle Lane
Punky Brewster

Quantum Leap
Quincy M.E.
Rainbow
Rainbow Brite
Record Breakers
Red Dwarf
Remington Steele
Rentaghost
Roseanne
Rumpole of the Bailey
Russ Abbot's Madhouse
Sale of the Century
Sapphire & Steel
Saturday Night Live
Saturday Superstore
Saved by the Bell
Screen Test
Sesame Street
She-Ra: Princess of Power
Simon and the Witch
Ski Sunday
Smith & Jones
Sons and Daughters
Sorry!
Spitting Image
Stig of the Dump
Stoppit and Tidyup
Street Hawk
Super Gran

SuperTed
T.J. Hooker
Taggart
Take Hart
Take the High Road
Tales of the Unexpected
Tenko
Terrahawks
Terry & June
That's Life
The Adventure Game
The Adventures of Teddy Ruxpin
The Amazing Adventures of Morph
The A-Team
The Basil Brush Show
The Benny Hill Show
The Children of Green Knowe
The Comic Strip Presents
The Dick Emery Show
The Dukes of Hazzard
The Flumps
The Flying Doctors
The Golden Girls
The Goodies
The Jetsons
The Keith Harris Show
The Krankies Elektronik Komik
The Krypton Factor
The Late Late Breakfast Show

The Laughter Show
The Les Dawson Show
The Les Dennis Laughter Show
The Littlest Hobo
The Magic Roundabout
The Moomins
The Morecambe and Wise Show
The Muppet Show
The Mysterious Cities of Gold
The Onedin Line
The Paul Hogan Show
The Price is Right
The Real Ghostbusters
The Rockford Files
The Secret Diary of Adrian Mole Aged 13¾
The Simpsons
The Smurfs
The Snowman
The Sooty Show
The Sullivans
The Thorn Birds
The Tripods
The Two Ronnies
The Val Doonican Music Show
The Waltons
The Wide Awake Club
The Wind in the Willows
The Young Ones
Thomas the Tank Engine and Friends

Three of a Kind
Through the Keyhole
Thundercats
Tiswas
To the Manor Born
Tomorrow's World
Tom's Midnight Garden
Top Gear
Top of the Pops
Transformers
Treasure Hunt
Tucker's Luck
Ulysses 31
University Challenge
Wacaday
Wheel of Fortune
Why Don't You (Just Switch Off Your Television Set and Go and Do Something Less Boring Instead)?
Willo the Wisp
Wizbit
Worzel Gummidge
Yes Minister
You Rang, M'Lord?

Films of the 1980s

A Fish Called Wanda	1988
Airplane	1980

Any Which Way You Can	1980
Arthur	1981
A View to a Kill	1985
Back to the Future	1985
Batteries Not Included	1987
Beetle Juice	1988
Beverly Hills Cop	1984
Big	1988
Biggles	1986
Bill & Ted's Excellent Adventure	1989
Caddyshack	1980
Chariots of Fire	1981
Clockwise	1986
Cocktail	1988
Cocoon	1985
Coming to America	1988
Crocodile Dundee	1986
Crocodile Dundee II	1988
Die Hard	1988
Dirty Dancing	1987
Dirty Rotten Scoundrels	1988
Driving Miss Daisy	1989
Educating Rita	1983
Empire of the Sun	1987
E. T. The Extra-Terrestrial	1982
Fatal Attraction	1987
Ferris Bueller's Day Off	1986
Flashdance	1983
Footloose	1984

For Your Eyes Only	1981
Ghostbusters	1984
Ghostbusters II	1989
Honey I Shrunk the Kids	1989
Indiana Jones & the Last Crusade	1989
Indiana Jones & the Raiders of the Lost Ark	1981
Indiana Jones & the Temple of Doom	1984
Labyrinth	1986
Lethal Weapon	1987
License to Kill	1989
Mannequin	1987
National Lampoon's Christmas Vacation	1989
National Lampoon's European Vacation	1985
Never Say Never Again	1983
Octopussy	1983
On Golden Pond	1981
Out of Africa	1985
Planes, Trains & Automobiles	1987
Police Academy	1984
Police Academy 2	1985
Police Academy 3	1986
Police Academy 4	1987
Police Academy 5	1988
Police Academy 6	1989
Private Benjamin	1980
Rain Man	1988
Raise the Titanic	1980
Robocop	1987
Romancing the Stone	1984

Roxanne	1987
Santa Claus: The Movie	1985
See No Evil, Hear No Evil	1989
Shirley Valentine	1989
Short Circuit	1986
Short Circuit 2	1988
Splash	1984
Stand By Me	1986
Teen Wolf	1985
The Blues Brothers	1980
The Breakfast Club	1985
The Burbs	1989
The Cannonball Run	1981
The Fly	1986
The Goonies	1985
The Karate Kid	1984
The Karate Kid Part II	1986
The Karate Kid Part III	1989
The Living Daylights	1987
The Man with One Red Shoe	1985
The Man with Two Brains	1983
The Money Pit	1986
The Naked Gun	1988
The NeverEnding Story	1984
The Tall Guy	1989
The Terminator	1984
This is Spinal Tap	1984
Three Men and a Baby	1987
Throw Momma from the Train	1987

Top Gun	1986
Trading Places	1983
Turner & Hooch	1989
Twins	1988
Uncle Buck	1989
Vice Versa	1988
Wall Street	1987
War Games	1983
Weird Science	1985
When Harry Met Sally	1989
Who Framed Roger Rabbit?	1988

Five

TOYS AND GAMES

If your parents are to be believed, the children of their generation had nothing more to play with than a single broken marble and a small piece of lint. Apparently, they had it tough in their day and they never had all the fancy toys we were blessed with when we were growing up. And they didn't get toys at Christmas either – instead, they were given a satsuma and a clip round the ear, and on special occasions, such as birthdays, the whole family would simply gather round the wireless to listen to the shipping forecast as a special treat. They were poor but they were happy.

Not so my generation. We were materialistic and greedy and we wanted more toys and better toys. We had so many toys we didn't know where to put them all. I remember our next-door neighbours used to clear out all the old toys each year and take them to the tip to make space for the new toys that would arrive at Christmas.

The 1980s was a period when children were spoiled like never before and the number and variety of toys available to children was greater than at any previous point in history. We not only had the cool new eighties toys to choose from, but we still had most of the toys from the sixties and seventies as well, like Space Hoppers, Stylophones, Meccano, Fuzzy-Felt, Play-Doh, Scalextric, Pogo Sticks, Spirographs, Stickle Bricks and Weebles (they wobble but they don't fall down). In fact, most of the toys we played with in the eighties were toys from the sixties or seventies, but as the decade wore on, an increasing variety of eighties toys were added to the mix.

Let's take a rummage through the toy cupboard of a typical 1980s child and see what retro treasures we can find.

Big Trak

If you were a 9-year-old child given the task of delivering an apple to your father, how would you choose to do it? Would you a) simply walk over to him and hand him the apple, or would you b) get out your Big Trak robotic transporter toy, programme in a sequence of commands and then watch with glee as the Big Trak delivered the apple in its trailer to your father, before shooting the cat with its built-in photon cannon? I think the answer to that question is fairly obvious. After using the Big Trak for the first couple of times you quickly realised that it took so long to programme the sequence of commands

Big Trak from MB Electronics – possibly the best toy in the world, ever.
(Courtesy of Martin Ling / Tomhannen / Wikimedia Commons)

that your dad had given up waiting, and anyway, the
chances are you would enter a wrong instruction in the
commands and send the Big Trak hurtling off in completely the wrong direction.

Nonetheless, Big Trak was highly entertaining and
actually pretty advanced for its time, storing a sequence
of up to sixteen commands which were programmed
in through a keypad on its roof. It had a series of direc-
tional arrows and numbers plus a few other buttons
for things like firing the photon cannon and pausing
the vehicle. It was even considered educational and my
primary school bought one to teach the children basic
programming and control, before realising that none of

the teachers could figure out how to operate it just like they couldn't work the Betamax video recorder or the school computer. The children picked it up in no time, though, and had the Big Trak patrolling the school corridors and noisily annihilating teachers with its photon cannon, which was really just a light bulb under a piece of blue plastic.

Though I was desperately hoping to get a Big Trak for Christmas, I never got one and only ever got to play with the one at school or at my friend's house. I'm still hoping I might get one for Christmas because in 2010 the Big Trak was re-released. And you know the first thing I'd do if I got one? Teach my children how to deliver me an apple!

Rubik's Cube

The Rubik's Cube was irritatingly difficult to solve, wasted huge amounts of precious playtime and encouraged smug smart alecs to watch your feeble attempts and then tell you how they could complete the puzzle in under three minutes.

It was created by Ernő Rubik, a Hungarian sculptor and professor of architecture; it measures 2.25 inches on each side and consists of a 3x3x3 assortment of twenty-six coloured squares. The aim is to unscramble the assorted colours by twisting the rows of squares around, so you eventually end up with a single colour on each side. The original Rubik's cube was invented in 1974 and was called the 'Magic Cube', but it wasn't until the puzzle was licensed to the Ideal Toy Corp in 1980 that it really rose to fame and quickly became the world's top-selling puzzle game.

I was one of the many frustrated children who spent countless hours trying to solve the cube, achieving no more than two completed sides; I even resorted to peeling off the stickers and swapping them around to make it look like I'd done it. However, a number of children managed to solve the cube with ease and went on to take part in speedcubing competitions to see who could complete the cube the fastest. In 1982 the Rubik's Cube World Championship was held in Budapest where the assembled crowds witnessed a 16-year-old boy solve the cube in just twenty-three seconds. Since then, the record has been broken over and over again, currently standing at just 7.08 seconds, set in 2008 at the Czech Open. Other crazy cube competitions have featured contestants solving the puzzle underwater, blindfolded and even using their feet! The year 2008 also saw the Guinness world record being set for the most people solving a Rubik's cube at one time – ninety-six people.

The massive commercial success of the Rubik's Cube inspired a whole range of new puzzles to be launched under the Rubik's brand name, including Rubik's Snake, Rubik's Magic, Rubik's Clock and Rubik's Revenge, but based on my experience of the original puzzle I decided to give all of these a miss.

Paul Daniels Magic Set

Cast your mind back to a time when Paul Daniels was popular. Not only was he curiously popular, but his magician's skills were unrivalled and millions of us would tune in each week to watch his TV programme (*The Paul Daniels Magic Show*, 1979–94) just to catch a glimpse of a new trick. There was no David Blaine-style freak-out street magic, no Derren Brown mind control, and no Penn and Teller showmanship; they were just straightforward tricks performed by a middle-aged man in a wig, telling bad jokes between illusions.

In a stroke of marketing genius, it soon became possible for every Paul Daniels fan to emulate their favourite magician when the Paul Daniels Magic Set hit toy stores up and down the UK. The box claimed it contained '150 magic tricks', however, nothing could have prepared you for the disappointment of tearing into your box on Christmas morning only to discover a measly rope, a set of plastic balls, a few thimbles, some playing cards, a wand, some plastic discs and two die. What, no Debbie McGee?

Fortunately, there was an instruction booklet included to help you make some sense of it all, but boy did it require practice if you had any chance of becoming the next Paul Daniels. Those who stuck with it and practised for hours mastered enough tricks to impress the family and all the kids at school. Sometimes you could even get a stand-in Debbie McGee to assist in the show, although, unlike Paul, I never tried sawing any of my assistants in half.

Thanks to the Paul Daniels Magic Set, I have now learned how to become that lovable fake-uncle figure that can pull coins out of children's ears. If only children were impressed by that sort of stuff these days.

Lego

I guess you could call me old-fashioned but I couldn't hide my disappointment recently when I discovered my daughter making a beautiful house made of Lego … on the computer. Instead of playing sprawled out on the carpet surrounded by a mountain of small plastic bricks, she was sat comfortably in a chair pushing around 'virtual' Lego with the click of a mouse. While the computer helped her create a stunning Edwardian mansion house, complete with beautiful landscaped grounds, she didn't get to experience the memorable childhood pain of kneeling on tiny pieces of Lego or the sense of achievement that comes from building an ugly, lopsided, multi-coloured box vaguely resembling a bungalow.

Having graduated from spiky plastic Stickle Bricks at an early age, I moved on to Duplo Lego, the large and difficult-to-swallow bricks designed for small hands, and became adept at building enormous towers that reached almost to the ceiling. By the age of 5, I was ready to move on to 'proper' Lego with its enormous array of pieces including bricks, windows, doors, roof tiles, furniture, people, animals, vehicles and basically anything you could possibly think of that you might conceivably require to build your own miniature model town.

After filling the living room with veritable cities of Lego, my parents decided to challenge me with the new Lego Technic sets that included more complicated mechanical parts like gears, axles, pins, beams and even pneumatic pieces and electric motors. For my 9th birthday I was given a Lego Technic car kit that contained all the pieces you needed to make a fully working scale model of a motor car, with a working rack and pinion steering system, coil spring suspension, forward and reverse gearbox and an electric motor with remote control unit. Thanks to Lego I not only enjoyed many happy hours of play, but I also learnt some fundamental principles of engineering and general mechanics.

Simon

In the mid-1970s, Atari came up with what it thought was another sure-fire arcade game success story. They innocently named it Touch Me, but the problem was few people ever did, because the actual game stank. However, a few years later, like a phoenix from the ashes, the idea rose again, and this time it was a success. Perhaps it had something to do with the new name, Simon (like Simon Says), because the game itself was still pretty dubious. Milton Bradley's version followed Atari's example, having four different coloured lights that flashed in varied sequences which players had to remember and then copy. After its launch at the *place du jour*, Studio 54 in New York, in 1978, Simon more than earned its place in pop culture and became the must-have Christmas present for that year.

The game, invented by Ralph H. Baer and Howard J. Morrison, was one of the earliest examples of microchip technology being used outside of computer gaming. You could choose from three levels of gaming to match your

An original MB Simon game, although you would be forgiven for thinking it was a smoke detector. *(Courtesy of Ian Falconer/Wikimedia Commons)*

level of memory prowess: Standard Simon, Challenge Simon or Group Simon. The premise was very similar with each level. Simon would light up the buttons in a random sequence and the players would have to remember the sequence and play it back correctly by pressing the buttons in order. You could set the difficulty levels to control the length of the sequence and also the speed at which they flashed. But if you hit a wrong button when playing back the sequence, Simon would express his disappointment by blowing a soul-destroying electronic raspberry. Then it was back to the beginning.

Perhaps the most bizarre aspect of Milton Bradley's marketing campaign was that Simon was directed towards middle-class suburbia as the ideal game to play after a sophisticated dinner party. Since when did flashing lights and surging adrenaline levels go well with cheese and pineapple on sticks? Instead, most people preferred to picture the game as educational – helping to improve hand-to-eye coordination and, of course, memory.

Over the years, the game's design hasn't really altered; it still looks like a smoke detector and has remained as chunky as always. Yet there is something about its colourful (red, green, blue and yellow) iconic design that makes it a winner. In 1979 Milton Bradley released the eight-buttoned Super Simon so players could try to outdo each other at the same time; later came Pocket Simon for the truly addicted.

Hungry Hungry Hippos

Ah, now here's a classy game of skill. Or make that blind panic and frantic arm-waving. If there was ever a game designed to warn children about the dangers of the ailment now known as RSI (Repetitive Strain Injury) then Hungry Hungry Hippos was it.

But physical pain was never enough to stop children playing; in fact, it made us play more. After all, Hungry Hungry Hippos was not so much about seeing who could feed their hippo the most, but rather about whose wrist could hold out the longest (which in the end meant the same thing).

Hungry Hungry Hippos, which was first produced in 1978 by Milton Bradley, consisted of a plastic moulded dish-like board with various nooks and crannies. On each of its sides nestled a plastic hippo – one green, one yellow, one pink and finally an orange one. The most unnatural thing about these hippos (as if their colouring wasn't enough) was the black levers sticking out of their rear ends. Once the Gamesmaster had emptied the hippo food (small white balls) into the centre of the board, each player had to push frantically on his or her hippo's lever in order to make the hippo open and close its mouth. The aim was to grab as many balls as possible, which would roll through the hippo's mouth and into a collecting trough. Predictably enough, the person with the most balls won. The game invariably lasted, at the most, one whole minute and consisted of a blur of rainbow colours and more than a whiff of greediness.

There was, like most children's games, no real element of skill involved (maybe that's why Homer from *The Simpsons* likes playing it so much). It's all about luck. One commentator in the *New York Times* provided the perfect description: 'The object of the game is essentially to press your handle down again and again as fast as you can, with no rhythm, no timing, just slam-slam-slam as your hippo surges out to grab marble after marble from the game surface.'

View-Master

Kids of the noughties got their fix from a trip to the IMAX cinema; kids of the nineties would crowd into a vomit-inducing simulator at the seaside; and kids of the eighties held coloured sweetie wrappers against their eyes. What are we talking about? The quest for 3D effects, that's what. OK, so not all kids had to resort to sweet wrappers back in the eighties – if they were very lucky, they had a View-Master.

Iconic in its design, everyone remembers the clunky red plastic GAF 'Model J' Viewer that had us all oohing and aahing. It was our first foray into virtual reality, after all. Basically, the View-Master was a device on which you could view slides of your favourite cartoons by inserting a paper disc and rotating it round with a click of the switch. There were all kinds of discs produced for the View-Master, from educational wildlife sets, the Seven Wonders of the World and even a twenty-five-volume anatomy of the human body, through to tales of Popeye and Doctor Who, Star Trek, The Man From U.N.C.L.E., Here's Lucy and The Beverly Hillbillies. Each frame also featured a line of text to give a bit more depth to the stories. It was wonderful, apart from when the unreliable trigger mechanism resulted in the frames not quite aligning.

The responsibility for the View-Master lies with a photography buff named William Gruber. In 1939 he envisioned a contraption which could take a slide, consisting of two overlapping images, that when looked at through two eyepieces would present a three-dimensional picture. During a visit to the Oregon Caves National Monument, Gruber met a man called Harold Graves who was the president of Sawyer's Photographic Services. Graves saw the potential of Gruber's stereoscopic camera rig and a partnership was formed between the two men. Shortly afterwards they produced the first prototype of the red wonder we all know and love. It was an instant hit.

When America went to war in the early 1940s, the military took an interest in the devices as a cheap way to train troops. They purchased a staggering 100,000 View-Masters and over 6 million reels. In 1951 Sawyer's acquired the Tru-Vu Company, their main competitor. This deal included the rights to their stereochrome viewers and, more importantly, the right to show Disney characters. Soon, kids everywhere were begging for a View-Master. In 1966 a company called the General Aniline and Film Corporation (or GAF) purchased

A red GAF View-Master – Model G to be precise. *(Courtesy of ThePassenger/ Wikimedia Commons)*

Sawyer's invention. A maker of Super 8 film and slides, they were able to license the rights to dozens of films and TV shows over the next two decades. With a heavy slant towards tourism still remaining, attractions such as Universal Studios, Marineland and the Detroit Zoo were also quick to produce discs.

The View-Master reached its peak of popularity in the early 1980s when it went hand in hand with all the 3D programmes TV channels were clamouring to broadcast at the time. Remember getting those red and green plastic glasses free with your weekly comic or copy of the

TV Times? They're probably still stuck down the side of some people's sofas.

Since 1939, twenty-five variations of the View-Master have been rolled out, including a Talking View-Master, various different-coloured designs, and 1.5 billion discs have been produced. The View-Masters are still popular today, although in 2008 Fisher Price announced it would cease producing slides of tourist attractions. Luckily for us, it would continue with its range of animated character slide sets. We can't wait to see what's next …

Madballs

'Catch them if you dare!' went the slogan. And very apt it was, too, for these bouncy little balls were the most grotesque and disgusting things you had ever clapped eyes on. They were, therefore, an instant hit – particularly with little boys.

Madballs were rubber balls measuring approximately 3 inches in diameter and decorated with disfigured, monster-like faces. They were the brainchild of AmToy which unveiled a range of eight 'characters' in 1985, promising that their grossness would not affect their bounciness as a ball.

Each Madball was its own little character, so they were instantly collectible. The range included Screamin' Meemie, Slobulus, Aargh, Hornhead, Dustbrain (a time-ravaged mummy), Oculus Orbus (who was basically one large bloodshot eye), Skull Face and Crack Head (who had his brains exposed). Due to their popularity a second series was released, including Badballs: Wolf Breath, Bruise Brother and Lock Lips. This was followed up with a range called Super Madballs, and later still some sports-themed Madballs joined the ranks. One of these was Foul Shot, who suffered from worms in his eye. As time went on, the grosser and more goo-filled they became.

The toys became so popular that they got their own animated TV series, a run of comics from Marvel/Star, and a video game for the ZX Spectrum, Amstrad CPC and Commodore 64.

While kids' greed for all things disgusting kept growing, Madballs just couldn't keep up, and they eventually lost their bounce. But that doesn't mean they've been forgotten. Some may still have nightmares about them …

Cabbage Patch Kids

Being a little boy in the 1980s with two brothers and no sisters, I had absolutely zero interest in or awareness of girls' toys and was sheltered from the mere existence of Barbie, Sindy or any other dolls of the time. However, my blissful ignorance of girls' toys was shattered in 1983 by the much-hyped arrival of the ugly, and yet insanely popular, Cabbage Patch Kids.

The Cabbage Patch Kids were a collection of dolls that originally began life in 1978 as part of an art exhibition, where their creator, Xavier Roberts, offered them up for adoption. He later began selling the dolls at Babyland General Hospital in Cleveland, Georgia, which was an old clinic converted into a shop. Roberts went the whole hog with this set-up, making everyone who worked there dress up and act as doctors and nurses, making sure that they cared for the dolls as if they were real children that had just been born.

The dolls themselves were ugly with podgy round faces, stumpy arms and small, close-set eyes; a computer-controlled manufacturing process randomly made small changes to each doll so that no two dolls were the same. The doll came complete with an adoption card, which the new owner would send off with their details, and on the first birthday of the doll, a card would be sent from the manufacturers.

The toys became immensely popular and began to attract media attention which, in turn, boosted their popularity further, until the toys achieved 'craze' status in the run-up to Christmas 1983. The first time I became aware of the Cabbage Patch Dolls was when I watched *John Craven's Newsround* and learned of the riots and fist fights occurring in shops across America as desperate parents literally fought each other to get their hands on the limited supply of dolls for their children. In fact, one 'crazed maniac', as described by the toy store owner, said she had travelled hundreds of miles to get the doll and she didn't even have any children! Another man, unable to get the dolls in America, flew to London especially to buy some for his daughter.

Thanks to the Cabbage Patch Kids I learned two important lessons at a very young age: first, never under-estimate the power of marketing; and second, never underestimate the danger of a mother on a mission.

Domino Rally

The television advert for Domino Rally featured several well-groomed children cheering and punching the air with uncontained excitement as their elaborate domino display toppled and rattled over a series of obstacles, including bridges, loop-the-loops, a flight of stairs and ultimately a launch pad that catapulted a plastic rocket in the air.

What they didn't show in the advert was the same well-groomed children laboriously setting up the hun-dreds of flimsy plastic dominos, one at a time, holding their breath and sticking out their tongues with the immense concentration required to prevent the dominos from falling over and destroying hours' worth of work prematurely. They also didn't show the rough edges of the dominos left over from the injection moulding proc-ess which made them inherently unstable and prone to spontaneous topplage.

If you could really be bothered to spend a gruelling and frustrating three hours setting up a Domino Rally display, you would be rewarded with a disappointingly brief demonstration that usually resulted in the Domino

Rally being packed away at the back of the toy cupboard and forgotten forever. It was far easier and more entertaining to watch the fruits of other people's labour on television shows like *Record Breakers* with Roy Castle and Norris McWhirter, where groups of students would set up millions of dominos in old aircraft hangars and set them off in colourful and intricate displays often recreating famous paintings, flags or scenes from around the world. Even the 'professionals' got it wrong sometimes and Norris McWhirter mournfully recounted the tale of hundreds of thousands of dominos being accidentally toppled after a photographer dropped his light meter at a record attempt in Japan.

Domino Rally was a short-lived craze thanks to the short attention span of most children, but the world record attempts for domino-toppling continue to this day.

Trivial Pursuit

When you were little and secretly watching your mum and dad host another soirée from the top of the stairs, that heady mix of prawn cocktail, Babycham and Trivial Pursuit seemed like the height of sophistication. In years to come, we all realised that neither prawn cocktail nor Babycham were the slightest bit sophisticated, but there was indeed something rather special about Trivial Pursuit.

Maybe it was something to do with the board game's classy racing-green packaging – the same as the iconic

MG sports cars, no less. Or the Trivial Pursuit logo emblazoned across the front as if with a quill. This is one game that isn't shallow by any means and has shown enough merit to keep generations playing, and learning, since it arrived on the scene in 1981.

Trivial Pursuit was one of the first trivia-based games to really flex our grey matter and give dear old Uncle Geoff a chance to shine in the sports and leisure round. As well as sports and leisure, which is signified by the orange places on the board, there are questions on geography (blue spaces), science and nature (green), history (yellow), entertainment (pink) and arts and culture (brown). When you land on a square, another player asks you a question corresponding to the colour of the space you are on. If you get it right, you keep going; get it wrong and it's the next person's turn.

A correct answer bags you what is affectionately known as 'a piece of pie', since each player has a plastic holder in which to place a segment of a circle – one for each trivia category – making it look like a pie. Once you've filled your pie, it's a race to the centre of the board to answer one final question and be crowned king or queen braniac.

Castle Grayskull

Castle Grayskull was the type of toy you really, really wanted, but probably didn't get. After all, it was big and expensive and the slime-green demon-skull fortress just didn't appeal to parents as much as it did to gore-loving 9-year-olds. Fortunately for me, my parents found a second-hand Castle Grayskull at a car-boot sale and gave it to my little brother for Christmas, so I got to battle my He-Man action figure against my brother's Skeletor figure on the ramparts of Castle Grayskull.

In the animated television series *Masters of the Universe*, Castle Grayskull was said to be located on the fictional planet of Eternia and was believed to contain secrets so powerful that whoever controlled the castle would control the whole of Eternia. Of course, everyone knows that baddies like powerful secrets and always try to rule the world, so Castle Grayskull naturally became a beacon to Skeletor and his evil friends, Hordak and the Snake Men, who spent most of their time tying to ambush the castle.

Fortunately, the much-coveted secrets in the castle were guarded by He-Man and his buddies. He-Man was the muscle-bound, basin-headed alter ego of Prince Adam who rode around on a green tiger called Battle Cat and hung out with the likes of She-Ra, moustachioed Man-at-Arms (proper name Duncan), and levitating elf-like thing Orko.

Although the Castle Grayskull toy was impressive and featured an elevator, a trap door, a cannon and a drawbridge, I never did discover any powerful secrets within its walls and I fear that my valiant efforts to defend it against the assault of my little brother and his Skeletor may have been a futile exercise.

Teenage Mutant Hero (Ninja) Turtles

Cowabunga, dude! Who didn't love playing with the 'Heroes in a Half Shell'? Michaelangelo, Leonardo, Raphael and Donatello were better known as the Teenage Mutant Ninja Turtles (and later the Teenage Mutant Hero Turtles so as not to look like they were encouraging violence in kids). Like most toys in the 1980s, they were action figures, complete with fully moveable plastic bodies and limbs that you could spend hours on end putting into poses. But they didn't start off like this.

Originally, the fearsome foursome were part of a humorous comic strip which was a parody of several other comics of the time. Created by Kevin Eastman and Peter Laird, the turtles lived in the sewers of New York, ate a lot of pizza and talked like they'd just hopped off a flight from Hawaii. The back-story goes that they started life as four regular turtles, who accidentally got covered in toxic waste which turned them into 6ft-tall mutations, hence the name Teenage *Mutant* Hero Turtles. Just like they were our heroes, the turtles had a hero of their own: Master Splinter, a rat with a knack for martial arts and wise words. Under Splinter's supervision, the foursome became great warriors, wearing bandanas in different colours to differentiate them, and they took on the likes of petty criminals around the city, as well as the infamous Shredder. A reporter called April was often on the scene and I think she quite fancied one of the turtles.

By the late eighties, the Teenage Mutant Hero Turtles had gained their own Saturday morning cartoon series, which was swiftly followed by the action figures so we could recreate episodes in our own living rooms. Each turtle came with their weapon of choice: Michaelangelo wore an orange bandana and carried nunchaku; Donatello wore a purple bandana and carried a staff; Raphael wore a red bandana and carried a pair of sai fighting knives; and Leonardo wore blue and wielded two samurai swords.

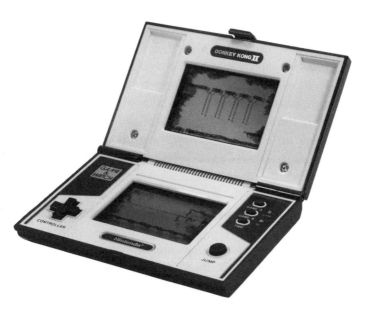

A Nintendo Game & Watch from 1983, featuring the Donkey Kong II game. *(Courtesy of Evan-Amos/Wikimedia Commons)*

Playmates Toys Inc. released a plethora of merchandise on top of this, including PEZ dispensers, skateboards, lunchboxes, toothpaste and even breakfast cereals. Then, in a move that rocked every kid's world in the nineties, a Teenage Mutant Hero Turtles film hit cinemas. As a result, the action figures range exploded, with even more variations of the main four (like turtles in disguise, where Michaelangelo got to realise his *raison d'être* by becoming a surfer), plus new characters like Bebo, who was a mutant pig, and Rocksteady, a mutant rhino. Accessories meant extended fun time, too, with the choice of a Sewer Party Tube and an armoured Party Wagon.

It was only when the Mighty Morphin Power Rangers hit the scene in the early 1990s that the turtles were forced back into the sewer. Nevertheless, in 2007 Turtle Power returned with another big-screen hit, and, having been a staple Happy Meal gift in the nineties, many a turtle can now be found at car boot sales.

Top Trumps

Does a V8 engine beat a V6 in Top Trumps? This was a debate that raged on in our household and has never been resolved to my satisfaction. If you were playing the Racing Cars pack then a V8 would definitely beat a V6 because it provided greater acceleration and overall power. However, if you were playing the Saloon Cars pack then you might argue that a V6 provided greater fuel economy and lower emissions in a lighter and more compact engine. My grandfather, an ex-racing driver, was called in to adjudicate on at least one occasion ruling in favour of the V6 (incorrectly so in my opinion).

The original Top Trumps games were launched in 1977 by a company called Dubreq and comprised a series of eleven different packs priced to be affordable to little boys with a few weeks' pocket money saved up. Each pack of Top Trumps was presented in a red plastic case with a clear lid and inside were around thirty cards, slightly larger than regular playing cards. Each card had a picture of the subject on it, be it a car or an aeroplane, for example, and a list of its vital statistics, like top speed, weight, length, horsepower and so on; the idea was to take it in turns to compare one of the statistics on your card with that of the other players. The player with the best statistic would win the other players' cards. In the event of a draw, the players would put their cards in a pile in the middle to be acquired by the winner of the next hand. Simple, really, and because of that simplicity, affordability and convenient pocket-size, Top Trumps became hugely popular, mainly with young boys who would take the cards to school to play in the playground.

Aside from the frequent arguments caused by ambiguous comparisons of values, I can safely say that Top Trumps was one of my favourite games in the eighties. Over the years I amassed a respectable collection of dozens of different packs, including military aircraft, tanks, motorbikes, warships, helicopters, hot rods, super dragsters, world airlines, rally cars, new spacecraft, experimental aircraft and all sorts of others. As the years went on the range of cards became more and more diverse and began to explore categories other than transport, eventually including such oddities as Millipedes and Centipedes (who has the most legs, I guess), FHM Cover Girls (not comparing the expected vital statistics) and Squirrel Trumps, where players compare the number of bird feeders destroyed, cats evaded and general fluffiness.

There were many more fantastic toys and games in my childhood than I'm able to cover in this one brief chapter and, while it's tempting to spend more time rummaging through our toy cupboard of the eighties, it really is time to continue. Let's press on and remind ourselves of the way the technology boom transformed our lives in the 1980s.

Six

TECHNOLOGY

It's been well over twenty years now since Michael J. Fox hover-skated around Hill Valley in *Back to the Future II* and I'm really disappointed I still don't have a hoverboard. Technology has given me a 3D BluRay HDTV, a Blackberry with Bluetooth, an iPad, an iPod and a thing in my car that goes beep to help me park, so why has no one been able to make a simple hoverboard? Back in the 1980s, I was certain that one day I would own a hoverboard because I was living in a decade where technology was advancing at such a rapid and exciting pace that it would surely only be a matter of months before someone had figured out how to make one. After all, this was the decade in which a man had flown a jetpack around the Olympic stadium in Los Angeles at the 1984 opening ceremony, so anything was possible.

While it turns out that no one was actually working on hoverboard prototypes, the technology industry had certainly been busy preparing all sorts of other exciting surprises for us and had seemingly been waiting until the 1980s began before unveiling all their new products at once. The technology assault began with the iconic arcade game Pac-Man, launching in Japan on 22 May 1980, closely followed by the equally iconic Sony Walkman in the USA just a few weeks later in June. This signalled the beginning of what was to become a relentless flood of new gadgets and devices throughout the eighties that, in most cases, owed their existences to the ever-increasing power and ever-decreasing price of the microchip.

The microchip (otherwise known as a silicon chip or integrated circuit) had been invented many years earlier in 1949 with the first working example produced in 1958. Partly as a result of well-funded US government space and defence departments that needed silicon chips for guiding their rockets, the price of microchips was gradually driven down to what was considered an affordable level for use in industrial applications, and it wasn't long before microchips were being produced in such high volumes that they became accessible to the average consumer. While microchips had already begun appearing in some homes in the mid-1970s, in the guise of digital wristwatches and early Atari consoles, the real technology boom began in the 1980s as the commercial potential of the microchip was increasingly realised. Now, thanks to the low price and high power of the microchip, I was able to use coupons from a cornflakes packet to buy a digital wristwatch that not only told the time, but also played the James Bond theme tune to promote the 1985 film *A View to a Kill*.

Of course, it wasn't all about the microchip and plenty of other new technologies emerged in the eighties completely independently of the electronics boom, such as the high-speed TGV train that launched in France in 1981. But if you ask most people what they remember about technology in the eighties, they will reel off long lists of electronic devices with scarcely a mention of anything else. Think about it: what comes to mind when you look back at 1980s technology? It's probably not the Hepatitis B vaccine that was invented in 1980 or the soft bifocal contact lense invented in 1983. Chances are you are thinking of electronic devices like VCRs, camcorders, Walkmen and microwave ovens. The rest of this chapter is unashamedly devoted to a handful of the, mostly electronic, technologies I remember fondly from my childhood in the eighties.

My recollection of the 1980s technology boom begins in 1981 when I watched an episode of the hugely popular BBC TV programme *Tomorrrow's World*, which showcased exciting developments in the world of technology and science. While every episode was an enthralling spectacle of gadgetry and live demonstrations that often failed, this particular episode was more memorable than most thanks to the Compact Disc or CD. Presenter Kieran Prendiville introduced us to this remarkable new technology for the first time and explained that not only was the Compact Disc far smaller than the standard

The very first Macintosh computer from Apple launched in 1984 with a $1.5 million TV advert directed by Ridley Scott. *(Schlaier/Wikimedia Commons)*

vinyl discs currently being used, but they were far more durable. To prove his claims, Prendiville took a brand-new Bee Gees CD and smeared it with strawberry jam before demonstrating that it could still be played in a CD player. The falsetto warbling of the bouffant, hairy-chested, medallion-wearing singers could clearly be heard despite the slathering of strawberry jam and, while their trapped-testicle voices made it sound like the CD player was malfunctioning, it was actually an accurate reproduction of the original recording.

The CD was the first of several nails in the coffin of the vinyl record, which was in comparison bulky and fragile with a tendency to warp and scratch. CDs were much smaller and tougher and boasted the remarkable ability of being able to change tracks almost instantly and even play in a random order if necessary. To fully appreciate just what a giant leap forward in technology this was at the time, you have to cast your mind back to the 1980s and imagine you are trying to locate your favourite song on the mix tape you have recorded off the radio: fast forward for ten seconds and press play. Not far enough. Fast forward another ten seconds and press play. Too far, you're in the middle of the song. Rewind for five seconds and press play. You've gone too far the other way now. This time you hold the play button halfway down as you press the fast forward button at the same time and hear high-speed Alvin and the Chipmunk-style renditions of eighties classics until you reach the point on the tape you were aiming for. At last, you press the play button and settle down to listen to your favourite track, *Agadoo* by Black Lace. However, after a few seconds you hear a strange rustling sound coming from the cassette player and on opening the door you discover a rapidly growing pile of thin black tape spewing out of the cassette and tangling around the rotating wheels.

Not only did the CD put an end to these nightmare scenarios, it also meant you could now listen to your music without the crackles and pops that you would get from vinyl or the hiss and distortion of cassettes. You could whack the volume right up and press play and have the music instantly burst out of your speakers with a clarity that was previously unheard of.

Despite its debut on *Tomorrow's World* in 1981, it wasn't until 1982 that the first CD player was commercially available for well over £1,000 in today's money, and it was some years later still before most people had fully embraced the technology. Not only was the CD player relatively expensive, but it meant buying a whole new set of music on CDs and working out what you were going to do with all your old vinyl records.

While the CD was changing the way we listened to music at home, the arrival of the personal stereo in 1980 liberated us from sitting in front of our hi-fis and allowed us to listen to all our favourite music on the move wherever we were: at home, on the bus, walking home from school or secretly listening under the covers in bed when we were supposed to be sleeping. In order to fully appreciate just what a big deal this was for us back then, you have to remember that, prior to the arrival of the personal stereo, or Walkman as it became ubiquitously known, the closest most of us got to al-fresco music was the sound of an ice-cream van driving past. Now we could listen to our music *wherever* we liked, and not only that, we could listen to *whatever* we liked and as loud as we liked without our parents shouting at us to 'turn off that terrible racket'. The personal stereo was way more than just a portable music player and became an icon of eighties pop culture representing musical freedom and technological advancement.

In 1978 a very clever Japanese chap called Nobutoshi Kihara built the first Walkman for Sony co-chairman Akio Morita, who spent a lot of time travelling on business and wanted to be able to listen to his favourite operas while flying across the Pacific. I say 'built' and not 'invented' because a very clever German-Brazilian fellow called Andreas Pavel actually invented and patented the first personal stereo some six years earlier, which he called the Stereobelt. As you might imagine, there was quite a kerfuffle when Mr Pavel became aware of Sony's new 'invention' and a long battle followed which spanned twenty-three years, concluding with Sony paying a cash settlement estimated in the region of $10,000,000 and acknowledging Mr Pavel as the original inventor of the personal stereo.

While Sony was the first to the market with its Walkman, it wasn't long before a range of competing products arrived and I remember just how thrilled I was when I was given a bright red Bush personal stereo one Christmas. It came with a pair of large headband-type headphones with orange foam padding for the ears and it had graphic equaliser sliders on the side and a button called 'boost', or something similar that essentially toggled the device between sounding disastrously terrible and somewhat acceptable. Despite being a portable stereo player, it was a tad on the large side and when it was clipped to my waistband it nearly pulled my trousers down. An unusual 'feature' of my personal stereo was the way the pitch of the music changed in time with the movement of my walk. The slight jolt of each footstep would create a wobble in the music so that it sounded like a warped record and as the batteries gradually ran down, the music became slower and deeper and ultimately made the Bee Gees sound like they were singing in normal voices.

I remember my dad reading me an article in the *Daily Express* in the 1980s about how some day we would no longer go into music shops like Our Price and buy cassette tapes with music albums on them. Instead, we would take our Walkman into the shop, plug it into a machine on the wall and 'download' the individual songs we wanted directly onto our own blank cassettes. Well, they got the downloading bit right I suppose, but back then we just couldn't see how anything could surpass the cassette tape.

The huge popularity of the personal stereo meant that compact audio cassettes received a significant boost in sales, finally putting paid to their ageing predecessor, the eight-track tape. And while the audio cassette was in its heyday, the video cassette also entered its prime after a decade of preparation.

The video cassette first appeared in a commercial format in 1971 when Sony invented the U-matic system comprising an enormous wood-panelled video recorder with cassette tapes that were slightly larger than standard VHS cassettes. This was undoubtedly a very desirable piece of technology, but few people could afford the $1,395 price tag which equates to over $7,000 today. Over the next few years, more competing formats were introduced and prices were driven down to the point when, in the late 1970s, people began to buy, or more frequently rent, the still very expensive video equipment. The famous format war between Sony's Betamax system and JVC's VHS system meant that there were two competing video cassette formats for a number of years; Sony fought a brave battle but ultimately conceded defeat in 1988 when they finally gave in and began producing VHS recording equipment.

I remember the excitement of our first video recorder with great clarity. My dad returned home one day staggering under the weight of an enormous wood-panelled VHS recorder which looked like a very sturdy and solid piece of equipment indeed. The buttons were large and heavy and made a reassuring thud when pressed and it came with a plug-in remote control with a coiled cable and a protective dust cover to keep it in pristine condition.

My dad pushed the eject button to open the cassette tray and with a loud clunk and crash the top of the video recorder sprung open to allow him to insert a VHS cassette. He showed us how you could record live television and then noisily rewind it and play it back; how you could pause the picture and how you could watch pre-recorded films from the video rental shop. Every weekend we would rent a film from the shop in town and come home and watch it. Then we would rewind it and watch it again. Then we would go to bed, wake up early and watch it again before taking it back to the video shop. Unfortunately, the video recorder was so noisy on account of its durable construction that our early morning film sessions woke my parents up, with the loud clunk-whirr-clunk noise when rewinding the tape, alerting them to our repeated viewing of the ladies' shower scene in *Police Academy*.

One of the early RCA VHS camcorders. Imagine lugging this baby around with you on holiday. *(Courtesy of Darian Hildebrand)*

As the video cassette recorder (VCR) was taking its place in a growing number of households, Sony released the first consumer camcorder in 1983 which allowed people to record video footage that could be played back on their televisions. Prior to the invention of camcorders, the only way most people had been able to record moving pictures was by using old-fashioned and expensive cine cameras, which then had to be played back on a reel-to-reel projector. With a camcorder you could record your family holidays and watch them back on the television. Or, you could film a crazy professor time-travelling in a DeLorean, like Michael J. Fox did in *Back to the Future*. In fact, if you watch that scene in *Back to the Future* again, you'll get a good idea of what the first camcorders were like. They were huge shoulder-mounted things that made you look like you were filming an outside broadcast for the local news station.

Gradually, improvements in technology meant that the camcorders became smaller and more affordable, and before long they had become so popular and widespread that a whole new genre of television show emerged at the end of the decade where people sent in their funny home videos, mainly of people falling over. Although no one realised it at the time, this was the beginning of the YouTube generation where people started to film themselves instead of just watching other people on the television. All of a sudden, unsigned bands could produce their own low-budget/no-budget music videos using hideous pixelated transition effects, wannabe actors and singers could show off their talents and my brothers and I could record ourselves re-enacting Monty Python sketches.

YouTube was still twenty years away in the future so there was no easy way of sharing your home videos with the rest of the world yet, but that didn't stop us recording hours and hours of pointless nonsense on to little VHS-C cassettes that could only be viewed by putting them inside a special motorised VHS cassette adapter that you could play in your VCR. In fact, I still have a collection of these little tapes in a cupboard somewhere but have no way of watching them since I have neither the VHS adapter anymore nor a VCR to watch them on. Probably just as well really, since I imagine it would be painfully embarrassing and possibly incriminating watching these with my family now.

With all this talk about CDs, Walkmen, VCRs and camcorders, you would be forgiven for thinking that the technological advances of the 1980s were confined to the improvement of our home entertainment, but in fact this was just one aspect of a technology revolution that was touching virtually every aspect of our lives. The eighties was a time when the research and development of the previous decades came into fruition in a very visible and practical way.

Take, for instance, the telephone system which had remained largely unchanged since its introduction almost 100 years earlier. Sure, there were a lot more phones now and the switchboards had become automated, but basically the system was the same. You dialled a number and you spoke to someone at the other end. That was it; there was no need to change the system because it worked beautifully. Back in 1980 my parents still had one of those telephones with an old-fashioned circular dial on the front that you wound round to dial the numbers, and this was fairly typical of many households at that time. A few 'trendy' people had replaced their old phones with fancy schmancy Trimphones that had a digital warble for a ringer instead of a mechanical bell, and some show-offs had bought expensive answering machines, but that was about as advanced as it got.

Early in the 1980s, though, Sony and a number of other manufacturers began to shake things up when they introduced the very first cordless telephones for the consumer market. Awkward teenagers everywhere could now slope off to their bedrooms, taking the telephone with them, to have their grunted conversations in private rather than next to the telephone within earshot of their parents. What many teenagers didn't realise, however, was that the early analogue cordless phones could easily be listened in to by any radio amateur and their supposedly secret conversations were probably being overheard by their nosey next-door neighbour.

Until the introduction of the cordless telephone, if you wanted to have a telephone conversation you had to stand right next to the telephone or risk severe entanglement with the coiled cable if you dared to try walking while talking. Now you could walk around with the telephone and had the freedom to even take it outside and have a conversation in your garden if you wanted to. Of course, some people took this freedom to unpalatable extremes and started taking their cordless phone with them into the bathroom and would have conversations with friends or family while seated on the lavatory. They might have thought no one knew where they were, but the tell-tale echoey background noise gave the game away.

The cordless phone was a precursor to the mobile phone and it wasn't until people began using cordless phones that they realised just how useful it would be

Time to upgrade my mobile phone, I reckon. This stylish beauty is an AEG Telecar CD 452. *(Courtesy of Christos Vittoratos/Wikimedia Commons)*

if they could take their telephones out and about with them wherever they were. If you wanted to make a telephone call while away from home, you had to use one of the many red public telephone boxes dotted around the country. This was all very well if you found a telephone box that hadn't been vandalised and happened to have a big, old-fashioned ten pence piece with you, but otherwise you were stuck.

Fortunately, the technology industry was one step ahead and had already been thinking about this problem for some time, and by 1985 the necessary infrastructure was in place to launch the UK's mobile network. At a few minutes past midnight on 1 January 1985, the very first mobile phone call in the UK was made by fledgling telecoms group Vodafone, heralding the beginning of yet another technological revolution.

The first mobile phones were amazing pieces of equipment that were hugely expensive and even more hugely proportioned. Motorola's DynaTAC 8000X was over a foot long and weighed in at almost 2lb, with an original asking price of \$3,995. If you want to see an authentic DynaTAC in action, check out Gordon Gekko in the 1987 film *Wall Street*. Don't worry, you'll know it when you see it – there's no missing it!

Nokia's first mobile phone, the Mobira Senator, was even worse than the DynaTAC, comprising a telephone and separate base station that weighed in at 21lb altogether, although in fairness this was designed to be used in a car.

The prohibitive cost of the mobile phones themselves and the exorbitant call charges meant the mobile industry was initially patronised by wealthy yuppies, who saw the mobile phone as a status symbol, and big businesses that could justify the costs. For many businesses the benefits of being able to communicate with their employees wherever they were outweighed the enormous costs involved, but a lot of businesses still preferred to use pagers as a cheaper alternative. Pagers were introduced way back in the 1950s but it wasn't until the 1980s that they really reached the peak of their popularity – particularly in the USA. For some reason pagers never really caught on in the UK, but if you look at any 1980s American movie, it would seem that all business people wore pagers attached to their belt and were often paged at the most inappropriate times.

For some, the cheapest communication solution wasn't pagers or mobile phones but Citizen Band (CB) radios which cost nothing to use except the licence fee. Although CB radio had been widely used in America since 1945, the British government strangely refused to legalise CB radio on 27MHz until November 1981, after a series of high-profile public demonstrations. CB radio instantly became popular with truckers, farmers and taxi drivers, among others, who used the service for professional purposes; and a huge number of hobbyists took to the airwaves no doubt inspired by Rubber Duck and his friends from the 1978 film *Convoy* and the 1977 film *Smokey and the Bandit*. Throughout the 1980s CB radios became widespread and foreshadowed internet chat rooms which were to appear in the late 1990s. CB users would chat to strangers on a wide range of subjects and, in common with internet chat rooms, developed their own unique slang vocabulary. Each person on the CB radio had their own 'handle', which was their nickname, and seemed to spend a lot of time saying 'ten-four' which was an unnecessarily complicated way of saying 'yes' or 'OK'. To the uninitiated, an exchange of dialogue between two breakers (CB users) sounded like gibberish, but truckers in particular understood each other perfectly and knew that eyeballing a spliced seat cover could get them in trouble. If you're not sure what that means, do a bit of Googling for a guide to CB slang.

Another major step forward in telecommunications technology was the widespread adoption of the fax machine which had started to appear in businesses in the late 1970s and had become ubiquitous by the 1980s. Think about how many emails you get every day at work and then remember that businesses in the eighties were not using email yet and you may appreciate just how useful the fax machine was for sending documents around the world. Every office had at least one fax machine and it would be working round the clock sending and receiving important documents. To reduce ink costs, thermal printers became popular, using a heated printing head to 'print' on to heat-sensitive paper thereby completely eliminating the need for printing inks. The only trouble was that the thermal paper tended to fade rapidly and any text printed on the paper gradually vanished over the course of a few years.

OK, that's already too much information about fax machines because, let's face it, they're supremely dull in comparison to what was probably the single most important technological development of the 1980s – the Personal Computer (PC). I'm sure you'll be relieved to hear that I'm not going to provide you with a detailed history of the personal computer, although I could probably write a book on that subject alone. I'm one of those geeky guys that knows way too much about computers and I'm one of the few super geeks who has actually made the pilgrimage to the famous suburban garage in California now dubbed 'the birthplace of silicon valley'. Here, Mr Hewlett and Mr Packard began their electronic tinkering many years ago which ultimately led to the invention of the PC.

So I'll try to keep my inner geek in check now as I recollect a few of my memories of computers in the 1980s, starting with the Atari 2600, a kind of 1980s version of an X-Box. One of my friends had an Atari 2600 and this was the first time I had ever seen any kind of computer or computer game. The Atari comprised a large wood-panelled box with a slot to insert games cartridges and a socket for a joystick. You plugged the Atari in to your television and then played games such as Pong, Pac-Man and Breakout, and as far as I was concerned, this was the best thing in the world. I desperately wanted my own Atari right there and then but had to wait patiently until a kindly uncle bought us a ZX Spectrum some time later.

The Sinclair ZX Spectrum, or Speccy as it became known, was a small black box mostly comprising a built-in keyboard with keys made of rubber that wore out very quickly. Games were stored on audio cassette tapes and to load a game you would type LOAD and then press the play button on a cassette player connected to the Speccy. The screen would flicker with brightly coloured horizontal bars as a loud screeching and whistling noise was heard from the audio tape. Anyone who has ever used a ZX Spectrum will have the tape-loading screeches indelibly burned into their memories, and they will remember the frustration of having to wait for five whole minutes while Manic Miner loaded, only to find that thirty seconds from completion the screen would display the crushingly inevitable 'R TAPE LOADING ERROR' message that meant you had to start all over again.

Fortunately, you could usually fix this problem by simply adjusting the volume level on your cassette player and eventually you would get to play Jet Set Willy, Horace goes Skiing, Dizzy, Head Over Heels and hundreds of other classic computer games. There was even an early word processor for the Spectrum and most impressively a flight simulator, which I find truly amazing with hindsight given that the ZX Spectrum had just 48KB of memory and a 3.5MHz processor. Sadly, the Speccy wasn't built to withstand the destructive force of me and my two brothers and it wasn't long before we had worn out the rubber keys on the keyboard and had worked our way

I loved my old rubber-keyed Speccy. This is a 48KB model like the one I had in 1982. *(Courtesy of Bill Bertram/Wikimedia Commons)*

through numerous joysticks, largely thanks to the game Daley Thompson's Decathlon, which involved waggling the joystick from side to side as fast as it could go.

Our next computer was a ZX Spectrum 128K which was not only more powerful but featured a built-in cassette player. We had now also bought a special plug-in device called a Multiface that allowed us to apply POKEs which were a way of cheating in games. For instance, you could press a special red button on your Multiface and then type 'POKE 47196, 201' and this would give your character immunity in the game Knight Lore. The good folks at *Your Sinclair* and *Sinclair User* magazines provided us with new cheat codes each month and also gave us cover-mounted cassette tapes loaded with samples of new games.

My brothers and I began spending so much time playing computer games that my dad decided to implement a strategy to limit our computer use: the strategy allowed us to use the computer for the same amount of time that we spent reading an educational book. It was a nice idea but it didn't really work since we each had a reading log and would try to build up as much time as possible for playing computer games by pretending to read when we were, in fact, playing games silently in our bedroom. By this time we were also playing computer games at school on the new BBC Microcomputers which, like Betamax VCRs, totally confounded most of the teachers and yet were fluently operated by a class of 6-year-olds.

The BBC Micro was one of the first computers to appear in schools and was powerfully packed with a whopping 2MHz CPU and 16KB of RAM costing a tidy £235 in 1981. For those of you who don't understand geek speak, that means your home PC today is well over a thousand times more powerful than the BBC, and in relative terms, less than half the price. But despite its seemingly modest specifications, the BBC Micro was a hugely advanced personal computer for its time and was, without a doubt, one of the most influential computers of the eighties.

Since there was only the one computer at my first school, it was very much in demand and consequently each child had limited access to it. We would take it in turns to play semi-educational games such as the well-known Podd, which was meant to teach young children to use verbs. The game featured a strange character called Podd that looked like a tomato with a face. You had to complete the sentence 'Podd can …' by adding any one of 120 verbs, such as dance, sing, whistle, run, etc. and then watch as Podd demonstrated each of these actions with a rudimentary animation. The animations were extremely basic and many of them looked confusingly similar. I'm not entirely sure there was any real difference between Podd's walk, stroll, amble, meander, saunter and mince.

If you don't remember Podd, there's a good chance you'll remember Granny's Garden, and maybe you still suffer nightmares at the memory of the pixelated cyan face of the evil witch that would inevitably catch you at every turn. The idea of the game was to wander through the mysterious Kingdom of the Mountains solving puzzles and searching for the King and Queen and their missing children Tom and Esther. Along the way you would encounter a talking toadstool, numerous witch attacks and a sneezing Asian character called Ah-Choo, who needed your help to feed some baby dragons. I never actually completed the game and got bored of it because the witch kept eating me; instead, I would spend my computer time writing things like:

```
10 PRINT 'BUM'
20 GOTO 10
```

Before long the Amiga 500 and Atari ST were both released, competing directly with each other and both offering game play far more impressive than anything I'd seen on a Speccy or BBC. My dad was somehow persuaded to buy us an Amiga since I told him it would be used for educational purposes; he even bought me a dot matrix printer to go with it so I could write my school essays and print them out. Of course, the Amiga was rarely used for educational purposes and was instead used as the high-performance gaming machine that it was. The Amiga came with a built-in floppy disc drive that meant your games would load within seconds and it had a whopping 512KB of RAM expandable to 1MB that allowed for highly detailed graphics and rocking soundtracks. The Amiga was the last computer I owned in the eighties and was a fitting conclusion to a decade of countless technological achievements.

By the end of the 1980s we not only had really cool computers but we had CDs, VCRs, camcorders and mobile phones, too. Technology in the eighties had touched every area of our lives and changed the way we worked, communicated, listened to music and watched TV, even the way we ate (think of the microwave oven). And you know what? Technology also gave me the chance to have a go on a hoverboard after all. It wasn't quite what I was expecting, but thanks to my trusty Amiga 500 I got to ride a virtual hoverboard in *Back to the Future II* the computer game!

Seven

FAMOUS PEOPLE

How do you solve a problem like Noel Edmonds? I mean, he was clearly one of the most famous personalities of the 1980s in the UK but his celebrity status spans at least five decades, so does he really count as an eighties celebrity? His haircut and dress sense don't help with his classification either, since they have remained consistently timeless throughout his entire career, unrepresentative of any particular decade. And in terms of popularity, he's probably just as well-loved today as he was back in the seventies, but there's definitely something eighties about him. It's like Caramacs and Curly Wurlys. There's just something about them that seems retro, despite them still being available today. Mars Bars, on the other hand, have been around for even longer, but for some reason they never feel dated. Noel Edmonds is a Caramac in the world of celebrity and he is joined, in this regard, by many others whose long careers make it virtually impossible to neatly assign them to any particular decade.

So it is without apology that I present to you a hand-picked selection of famous people from the 1980s, some of whom are Caramacs and some of whom are Mars Bars. There are one or two Cadbury's Fuses here (people who were hugely popular for a few years and then disappeared without trace), but I'll start you off with an ice-skating couple I like to think of as Wispa Bars (big in the eighties, who then disappeared into obscurity before making a surprising comeback years later).

Torvill and Dean

British, European, Olympic and World champion figure skaters Jayne Torvill and Christopher Dean are widely regarded as the UK's most famous and successful ice dancers of all time. In 1984 they were relatively unknown until they performed their now-famous routine at the Winter Olympics in Sarajevo, Yugoslavia. The four-minute performance won them a standing ovation, a gold medal and a record-breaking score of twelve perfect sixes, and from that moment on Torvill and Dean became household names.

The pair first skated together in 1975 when they were paired up by their coach and they began winning competitions immediately. Before turning professional, the pair had to fit their demanding skating practice and competition schedule around their careers, since Jayne was an insurance clerk and Christopher was a policeman, both living in Nottingham. Things started to turn around for Torvill and Dean when they took on the actor and singer Michael Crawford (of *Some Mothers Do 'Ave 'Em* and Phantom of the Opera fame) as their mentor in 1981. Crawford gave them acting lessons in order to heighten the performance of their figure skating and tagged along with them to sit at the ringside during their famous Bolero performance.

To coincide with their ten-year anniversary as professional figure skaters, Torvill and Dean decided to return to professional championships for the 1994 Olympics in Lillehammer, Norway, where they performed a Fred Astaire and Ginger Rogers-esque *Face the Music* routine. Although they didn't sweep the boards with perfect 6.0s for this performance, they were placed at a respectable third place behind gold winners Grishuk and Platov (who ended up winning gold medals four years running).

Despite their disappointing finish and the realisation that they were no longer Olympic gold winners, Torvill and Dean set off on their own 'Face the Music' tour. Christopher Dean also choreographed a number of dances to the songs of Paul Simon for the English National Ballet and toured with the 'Stars on Ice' show. In 1998 they produced a show that was performed at Wembley Stadium called 'Ice Adventures'.

Torvill and Dean officially retired in 1998 and went their separate ways, working as coaches and choreographers.

However, in 2006 they were coaxed out of retirement by ITV to coach celebrities and choreograph dances for the TV show *Dancing on Ice*.

Barbara Woodhouse

I'm still slightly confused about Barbara Woodhouse. There's no doubt she was an interesting person and an experienced animal trainer, but quite how she managed to secure a BBC prime-time slot on Saturday evenings for her series *Training Dogs the Woodhouse Way*, I really don't know. Having spent most of her life as a horse trainer, dog breeder and kennel owner, she first appeared on television on the programme *What's My Line?*, a game show where panellists had to guess her occupation. Although they failed to correctly guess what she did, something about her indomitable, eccentric, schoolmistress personality seemed to appeal to the general public, or perhaps it was her tweed skirts and sensible shoes, I don't know. Whatever it was, she instantly became a hit and her weekly dog training TV show made her a household name in the early eighties.

Barbara Woodhouse was best known for her catchphrases 'Sit!' and 'Walkies!' both pronounced in the most forceful and frightening manner guaranteed to subdue her canine pupils as well as their owners. A stern hand gesture accompanied the 'sit!' command and if the dog's owners didn't perform the gesture correctly or pronounce the catchphrase forcefully enough they would be severely chastised by Mrs Woodhouse. In fact, I seem to remember Barbara Woodhouse spending more time training the dog's owners than she did training the dogs themselves, and she always explained that there were no such things as bad dogs, only inexperienced owners.

Having become something of a sensation with a reputation for being able to tame even the most badly behaved dogs (and their owners), Barbara Woodhouse was summoned to Hollywood to perform her magic on the pooches of the rich and famous, including those of Britt Ekland, Zsa Zsa Gabor, David Soul and William Shatner, among others. However, the highlight of her career, in my opinion, was when she was asked to advertise eggs for the British Egg Marketing Board. Barbara was filmed reclining in her armchair telling us to show eggs who's boss. She then violently attacked a boiled egg with a teaspoon as she reeled off the catchphrase, 'Go smash an egg!' Genius!

Rod Hull and Emu (and Grotbags)

My earliest memories of Rod Hull and Emu come drifting back to me from the children's television series *Emu's World*, in which Rod and a relatively sedate Emu would entertain a group of children visiting the Pink Windmill where the pair were supposed to live. Every week the doorbell would ring (or rather make a sneezing sound) and Rod Hull would chant the catchphrase, 'there's somebody at the door, there's somebody at the door', before opening it to find a green-faced, overweight witch called Grotbags who was intent on stealing Emu. Why he opened the door each week is anyone's guess since we all knew it was going to be Grotbags and her useless assistants: a cowardly crocodile unimaginatively named Croc and a robot butler rather strangely named Robert Redford.

Grotbags would proceed to terrorise the children by pointing at them with her 'bazzazzer', a gold-coloured fake arm with an umbrella handle at one end, activating it by shouting 'Bazzazz!' Fortunately, the bazzazzer was completely harmless and never inflicted any injury on the children, but it did double up as a kind of mobile phone for Grotbags, which was handy.

At this point I should backtrack a little and explain that prior to *Emu's World*, Rod Hull and Emu had been performing together since the early 1970s and had become highly successful with adult audiences as well as with children. The Emu puppet became well known for its highly aggressive personality that caused havoc when it attacked people without provocation; meanwhile, Rod would make a pantomime of trying to hold back the uncontrollable blue bird, often rolling on the floor or on top of the victim in the process. It was one of those things you watched with a mixture of horror and fascination and made you laugh nervously, wondering what the crazy man was going to do next. There seemed to be no boundaries for Emu's outrageous behaviour. Not only did Emu knock Michael Parkinson off his chair during an interview, he also destroyed the Queen Mother's bouquet of flowers during the after-show line-up at the Royal Variety Performance, and attacked Richard Pryor on *The Tonight Show* shortly after Pryor had undergone major emergency surgery. Not everyone saw the funny side of Emu, though, and Billy Connolly threatened to break the bird's neck and Rod Hull's arm if they came anywhere near him on the *Parkinson* show.

I had an Emu puppet as a child and would attack my brothers with it occasionally, but for some reason I never got away with it. If Rod Hull did it, everyone thought it was funny, but if I did it I got sent to my room. Not fair.

The Roly Polys

Imagine a group of five fat, middle-aged women dressed in sequined cabaret costumes singing and dancing badly to show tunes. No, seriously, just picture it for a moment. This was the image that hit television screens and stages across the country in 1982 after Les Dawson and Ernest Maxim dreamt up the act for a BBC television series. There was no accounting for their tremendous success which saw them become guest stars on countless television shows and led to a long-running career on stage supporting cabaret and comedy acts such as Cannon and Ball and Frank Carson.

Sylvester Stallone in 1983 sporting a pair of highly fashionable Aviator sunglasses. *(Courtesy of Alan Light/Wikimedia Commons)*

The larger-than-life ladies would skip, strut and tap dance their way across the stage, often incorporating elements of comedy, involving deliberate mistakes or improbable and unpleasant dance moves such as pelvic thrusts. Leading lady Mo Moreland became such a notable character in her own right that she was eventually the subject of *This is Your Life*.

Big Daddy and Giant Haystacks

If someone told you that you were going to have to wrestle with an overweight, middle-aged man in a leotard called Shirley Crabtree, you might be forgiven for thinking you had a decent chance of winning. But if you knew that Shirley Crabtree was the real name of Big Daddy, one of the best-loved British wrestlers of all time, you might want to think again. Dressed in his signature Union Jack jacket and glittery top hat, the 6ft 2in, 26 stone wrestler from Halifax was someone you really wouldn't want to mess with.

Big Daddy's arch rival was Martin Ruane, a 6ft 11in giant of a man weighing in at 48 stone, known in the wrestling world as Giant Haystacks, and the pair famously had a long-running feud which resulted in high ratings on ITV any time they battled each other. Wrestling mania swept the country in the 1970s and 1980s and attracted enormous viewing audiences of all ages. Even little old ladies would be seen at the ringside screaming at Big Daddy to pound his opponent to oblivion. Sadly, that's exactly what did happen in 1987, when Big Daddy delivered his trademark 'belly-splash' move on his opponent Mal 'King Kong' Kirk. Kirk never recovered from the belly-splash move and was rushed to hospital where he was pronounced dead on arrival. The inquest later found that Kirk's death was the result of an existing heart condition and while Big Daddy was cleared of any responsibility, he blamed himself for Kirk's death and bowed out of professional wrestling.

Big Daddy was seen a few more times into the early 1990s, mainly appearing in tag team matches, but he had removed his belly-splash move from the routine altogether and chose to simply stand firm as his opponents attempted to body-charge him, usually just bouncing off his enormous belly. Giant Haystacks continued to wrestle internationally under the ring name The Loch Ness Monster, or simply Loch Ness, until he became ill and died in the late nineties leaving an enormous haystack-shaped hole in the heart of the wrestling world.

Dave Lee Travis

Some remember him as DLT, some remember him as The Hairy Cornflake and some remember him as 'that bearded bloke from Radio One that resigned live on air'. However you remember him, Dave Lee Travis was one of the most popular Radio One presenters of the 1980s, hosting numerous different shows over the years. He was responsible for coining the catchphrase 'comin' atcha through the cornflakes', the bizarre sound effect 'quack quack oops!' and introducing the nation to the concept of radio snooker.

Personally, I remember him as the bloke that hosted the Radio One Roadshow in the eighties, touring the nation in a large truck with drop-down sides that doubled up as a stage. On the sides of the truck were the blue and red Radio One logo and the numbers 275/285, which was the station frequency at the time (they didn't broadcast on FM until 1988). A selection of mediocre musicians would tour with them and perform their latest hits on the truck/stage, while the disproportionately excited audience were supplied with Radio One hats, t-shirts and various other poptastic goodies.

It came as something of a surprise in 1993 when Dave Lee Travis resigned live on air, complaining about changes afoot at Radio One that he wasn't happy about telling listeners: '... and I really want to put the record straight at this point and I thought you ought to know – changes are being made here which go against my principles and I just cannot agree with them.' It turns out he was going to be retired in a few weeks anyway so it was probably a good chance to get in there first and pretend it was all his idea.

The Hairy Cornflake left Radio One with his big, hairy head held high and moved on to new pastures which included a spell at Classic Gold Radio followed by a brief stint working for the Army's Garrison Radio. He then spent a few years on BBC Three Counties Radio and a whopping twenty years presenting a show on the BBC World Service. The Burmese pro-democracy leader, Aung San Suu Kyi, who spent fifteen years under house arrest from 1989, told the BBC that Dave Lee Travis's show on the World Service had made her 'world much more complete'.

John Candy

Never has the phrase 'larger than life' been more appropriate than when describing John Candy, the plus-size, loveable Canadian actor. Born in 1950, Candy began acting at an early age and appeared in his first movies in the early 1970s in fairly low-key roles. By the early eighties, Candy's career was picking up and he was offered more significant roles in the films *Stripes*, *Heavy Metal* and *National Lampoon's Vacation*, before appearing in what many consider to be his breakout role as Tom Hank's womanising brother in the romantic comedy *Splash*.

Candy went on to appear in a number of successful eighties movies, including *Brewster's Millions* and *Little Shop of Horrors*, before co-starring alongside Steve Martin in the classic John Hughes comedy *Planes, Trains and Automobiles*. Candy plays Del Griffith, a talkative, travelling, shower-curtain ring salesman of no fixed abode who befriends Neal Page (Martin) during a business trip. The unlikely pair embark on a long-winded journey together in an attempt to get to Chicago in time for Thanksgiving, enduring numerous setbacks along the way, mainly thanks to the well-meaning but accident-prone antics of Griffith.

Two years later in 1989, John Candy starred in the under-rated comedy *Who's Harry Crumb?* as a bumbling and inept private investigator hired to look into a kidnapping case. But for me, Candy's defining role came in the same year when he played Uncle Buck in the eponymously titled film. *Uncle Buck* tells the story of Bob and his wife Cindy and their three children Tia, Miles and Maizy. Cindy's father is unwell and both Bob and Cindy need to spend a few days away visiting him so they desperately look for a babysitter to take care of the children; they finally agree to ask Bob's brother Buck to do the honours. With some trepidation, Bob and Cindy leave the children with Buck knowing that he is a lazy, unemployed gambler who smokes, drinks and earns a living betting on rigged horse races. Despite Buck's outward appearance, he has a heart of gold and looks after the children wonderfully in his own unique style. This involves taking the kids to Buck's favourite bowling alley, beating up a drunken clown at a child's birthday party and intimidating Tia's no-good boyfriend with a hatchet.

Miles, the middle child, is played by Macaulay Culkin in one of his earliest movie appearances, and it is his role in Uncle Buck that inspired the concept for the film *Home Alone*. Geeky film-spotters will notice numerous similarities between the two films which are both written by John Hughes. Not only is Macaulay Culkin's character extremely similar in both, but there are a number of scenes in *Uncle Buck*, including the interrogation scene and the letterbox scene, which are clearly reflected in *Home Alone*. In *Home Alone* John Candy's role as Gus Polinski 'the Polka King of the Mid-West' is clearly inspired by his earlier character Del Griffith from *Planes, Trains and Automobiles* (also written by John Hughes).

Somewhat typecast as a loquacious but lovable character, Candy went on to appear in a number of other films, but sadly his movie career was cut short when he died of a heart attack in 1994.

Ronald Reagan

Ronald Wilson Reagan was the fortieth President of the United States of America holding office between 1981 and 1989. Born in 1911, Reagan first worked as a radio broadcaster before starting his career as an actor, appearing in over fifty movies and becoming a well-known public figure prior to his involvement in politics. In 1967 he was elected thirty-third Governor of California, a role later filled by movie actor Arnold Schwarzenegger, and in the 1980 presidential elections he defeated incumbent Jimmy Carter, taking office on 20 January 1981 as the new President of the United States.

US President Ronald Reagan in 1983 doing a fine impersonation of his *Spitting Image* puppet. *(Public Domain)*

As president, Reagan introduced dramatic new political and economic initiatives, including the reduction of taxes to promote economic growth, the reduction of government spending and the deregulation of the economy. After only sixty-nine days as president, Reagan was nearly killed in an assassination attempt that left him, his press secretary James Brady, police officer Thomas Delahanty and Secret Service agent Timothy McCarthy seriously injured. Miraculously, Reagan survived the incident, as did all his colleagues, and he came to believe that God had spared his life so that he might go on to fulfil a greater purpose. As it happens, the incident had a great influence on Reagan's popularity polls which peaked at 73 per cent after the shooting and he went on to complete two terms in office.

Princess Diana

Very little introduction is needed for one of the most famous women of all time, Diana the Princess of Wales. Following her official engagement to Prince Charles on 24 February 1981, the blushing 19-year-old was wrenched from obscurity and thrust into the public spotlight. The wedding took place at St Paul's Cathedral in front of a congregation of 3,500, while 600,000 spectators lined the streets outside. This was dwarfed, however, by the 750 million viewers around the world who watched the event on TV, making it the most popular programme ever broadcast at the time.

Just months after the wedding Diana became pregnant and gave birth to her first son William on 21 June 1982; a second son, Harry, was born on 15 September 1984. What the public didn't realise at this stage was that Prince Charles's long-running relationship with Camilla Parker-Bowles was already putting a strain on his marriage to Diana and as the marital relationship broke down, so too did Diana's relations with the rest of the royal family.

Throughout her marriage to Charles, Princess Diana was heavily involved in charity work making countless appearances at hospitals, schools and other facilities, taking a particular interest in charitable work relating to serious illnesses such as AIDS and leprosy. She became well known for her compassionate nature and demonstrated a fragile and sensitive personality that was troubled by depression and eating disorders.

Her marriage to Prince Charles broke down irrevocably and in 1992 the couple announced their formal separation. Having become the most famous and photographed woman in the world, Diana found it impossible to escape the intrusion of the paparazzi and it wasn't long before her relationship with Dodi Al-Fayed hit the headlines, along with intimate photographs of Diana and Dodi together on holiday.

As we all know, the story had a tragic ending with Diana and Dodi being killed in a high-speed car accident in Paris on 31 August 1997, leaving the nation to mourn the loss of the 'people's princess'.

Cannon and Ball

Back in the 1980s, when Cannon and Ball had their own TV show, I remember thinking that they weren't particularly funny, but I was so young then I probably didn't get their jokes. It wasn't until many years later, when I looked back at their shows, that I discovered I was right all along – they're not particularly funny. I was never a fan, but some people obviously liked them because they had 17 million viewers at their peak and were the highest paid act in British comedy in the eighties.

The comedy double act met when they worked together as a pair of welders in Oldham, Lancashire. Bobby Ball did a bit of singing at the weekends and asked Tommy Cannon if he wanted to come along; soon enough Tommy became part of the act which evolved from a singing duo to the comedy double act that was so popular in the eighties.

A lucky break in 1979 meant they caught the attention of the right people at ITV who offered them their own television show which became an instant success. The duo became so popular that in 1985 their Summer Season outsold Bruce Springsteen's British tour and the pair were reportedly earning around £50,000 per week.

Viewers loved Bobby Ball's cheeky clowning antics and his famous catchphrase 'Rock on Tommy!' but Tommy Cannon always maintained a straight-man image and suffered severely in the popularity stakes as a result. I remember interviewing both Tommy Cannon and Bobby Ball in 2007 just before they appeared on *I'm a Celebrity, Get Me Out of Here!*. Tommy told me that he was very close to Bobby and the bullying antics he showed on staged were all part of the act, although some people didn't seem to realise that. Poor Tommy said that he'd had to endure forty-one years of audiences booing him, old ladies beating him up with their handbags and threats of violence from the crowd.

Towards the end of the eighties, the duo's popularity began to tail off as the new breed of alternative comics dominated the comedy circuit. The pair famously converted to Christianity in later years and set up their own Gospel Show which tours churches around the country, sometimes involving fellow Christian Syd Little, of Little and Large fame.

Nigel Mansell

Formula One motor racing is one of the fastest, most exciting and dangerous sports on the planet, requiring drivers with lightning-fast reactions, nerves of steel and boundless energy. So it came as something of a surprise when the Formula One racing scene in the 1980s was challenged by a newcomer in the shape of Nigel Mansell, whose famous Brummie monotone led to him being described by some as the most boring man in sport. Even reviewers of his autobiography complained that Mansell had managed to turn an exciting story into an incredibly dull read.

Whenever Mansell was interviewed outside of his racing car, his droopy moustache, caterpillar eyebrows and dreary voice gave the impression of a down-trodden, slow-moving man that you would never in a million years expect to be a racing driver. But once kitted up and strapped into his car, Mansell transformed into a highly competitive and determined racing driver with a killer instinct and a taste for victory.

In fact, he was so competitive and determined that when his Lotus broke down at the end of the 1984 Dallas Grand Prix, just a few hundred yards from the finish line, Mansell sprung out of the car and began to push it hoping to still score a championship point for a sixth place finish. Unfortunately, the race was one of the hottest on record and, having already endured two hours of racing in temperatures of around 104°F, Mansell fainted some way short of the finish line.

Nigel Mansell's Formula One racing career spanned fifteen seasons and his prowess on the track made him the most successful British Formula One driver of all time: he claimed a total of thirty-one victories and set the record for the most pole positions secured in a single season. He became Britain's highest paid sportsman and Sports Personality of the Year 1986, and was also the only person ever to become the Formula One World Champion and the Indy Car World Champion simultaneously.

Margaret Thatcher

Born in 1925, the daughter of a grocer, Margaret Thatcher was Britain's first female prime minister and served three terms in office between 1979 and 1990. Her controversial political philosophy emphasised deregulation, flexible labour markets, reform of the trade unions, privatisation of state-owned utilities and industries, and reduced social expenditure, but while her policies successfully reduced inflation, unemployment increased at an alarming rate.

A decline in popularity in the early 1980s was inevitable amid the backdrop of recession and growing unemployment, but signs of economic recovery and her handling of the 1982 Falklands War resulted in a resurgence of support from the public which contributed to her re-election in 1983.

Appropriately nicknamed 'the Iron Lady', Margaret Thatcher was clearly a force to be reckoned with and thanks to her sharp tongue, sizeable shoulder pads and no-nonsense attitude, she comfortably stood her ground in the male-dominated world of politics. She was so tough, in fact, that she seemed to be virtually indestructible, surviving on just four hours of sleep per night and staying awake for the entire three months of the Falklands War, with only twenty-minute catnaps and plenty of whisky to keep her going. She even survived an assassination attempt in 1984 when the IRA planted a bomb at the Grand Hotel in Brighton where she was staying for a conference. The bomb detonated in a nearby room killing five people but leaving Mrs Thatcher and her husband unscathed.

Mrs Thatcher was re-elected for a third term in 1987, but her hard-line implementation of the new Community Charge or 'Poll Tax' seriously damaged her popularity with the general public and her views on the European Community led to serious dissension within her cabinet. Following the resignation of the deputy prime minister, Geoffrey Howe, over Mrs Thatcher's refusal to give a timetable for Britain to join the European single currency, a challenge for the leadership of the Conservative Party was mounted by Michael Heseltine, which resulted in a ballot attracting sufficient support to threaten Mrs Thatcher's premiership.

Margaret Thatcher in 1981 returning from a visit to the United States. *(Public Domain)*

On 28 November 1990 a tearful Margaret Thatcher left 10 Downing Street for the last time and made a dignified speech thanking all her staff and wishing John Major 'all the luck in the world' as the new prime minister. Behind the scenes she was devastated and felt betrayed by her cabinet, but she immediately continued with her political career as a backbench MP for Finchley.

Kenny Everett

Controversial? Certainly. Loose cannon? Definitely. Kenny Everett was, without doubt, one of the most dangerous and risqué entertainers of the 1980s with a no-holds-barred approach to comedy and a notoriously unpredictable manner. Having been dismissed from Radio London for his outspoken criticism of their religious programming, he moved to Radio One and was dismissed again after making a joke about the British Transport Minister bribing her driving test examiner. He still did not learn his lesson and Kenny was dismissed a third time from Radio 2 after making a rude joke about Margaret Thatcher.

After making something of a name for himself in the world of radio, Kenny was offered his own television show in the late seventies called *The Kenny Everett Video Show*. This programme introduced us to some of his more memorable characters, including ageing rock star Sid Snot, pervy Frenchman Marcel Wave, and

Angry of Mayfair, a middle-class city gent who would complain about the risqué content of the show before turning his back and storming off, only to reveal that he was wearing women's underwear as the back half of his suit was missing.

Kenny moved to the BBC in 1981 and created *The Kenny Everett Television Show* which ran for seven years. For this show he included some variations of his old characters plus a number of entirely new characters, including one of his most famous creations, an American B-movie actress called Cupid, whose name was a rude spoonerism that I cannot repeat in full. Cupid had inflatable breasts, made no attempt to hide her beard and would cross her legs with a high kick to ensure her knickers were flashed to comic effect.

Everett's risqué style and track record made him a dangerous guest for live television and poor old Russell Harty was clearly nervous on his live chat show when Kenny began telling a dirty poem about a boy 'eating red hot scallops'. Fortunately, Kenny stopped at the crucial point but resumed the poem in the last moments of the show and, as the credits started to roll, shouted out the obscene conclusion.

Despite his reputation, a bizarre set of circumstances resulted in Kenny delivering a 'speech' at the 1983 Conservative Party Conference, wearing his trademark giant foam pointing hands. He shouted to the assembled crowds, 'Let's bomb Russia!' and 'Let's kick Michael Foot's stick away!', to which he received huge cheers from the audience. Everett then posed for photographs with a beaming Margaret Thatcher while still wearing his giant foam hands.

And what better way could there possibly be to close the chapter than with this surreal image in mind?

Eight

WORLD EVENTS

Thanks to *John Craven's Newsround*, I've got a pretty good recollection of all the major events that happened around the world in the 1980s. The daily, child-friendly news reports kept me up to date with all the most important happenings from around the globe and explained them to me in a way that was simple to understand without being patronising. *Newsround* was the first British television programme to report the loss of the Space Shuttle Challenger in 1986 and was the first to report the assassination attempt on Pope John Paul II in 1981. But as well as reporting on the tragedies, famines, wars and terrorism, *Newsround* showed us that good things were happening, too, and making the world a better place. *Newsround* told us about the fall of the Berlin Wall, the royal wedding between Prince Charles and Lady Diana, the World Land Speed Record attempt by Richard Noble and, for some reason, told us a disproportionately large amount about pandas.

Taking my cue from John Craven and the *Newsround* team, I have put together a selection of both the good news and the bad news that I remember from the eighties.

The Great Storm of 1987

Poor old Michael Fish – he's never going to live this one down, is he? On the evening of 15 October 1987 the nation watched Michael Fish deliver a reassuring weather forecast with the opening remark: 'Earlier on today, apparently, a woman rang the BBC and said she heard there was a hurricane on the way; well, if you're watching, don't worry, there isn't.'

Just a few hours later, Britain was ravaged by the worst storm in nearly 300 years, claiming the lives of at least eighteen people, causing an estimated £7.3 billion worth of damage and serving up a large portion of egg on Michael Fish's face. While the storm wasn't technically a hurricane, it certainly had winds of hurricane intensity, with speeds of up to 134mph recorded at its peak.

I remember going to bed that evening and hearing the roof tiles lifting off the roof, the howling of violent winds and the crashing of objects being hurled around outside. The storm continued through the night and in the morning the full extent of the damage was evident. Our house remained largely intact with just a few roof tiles missing, but the garden was decimated with plants flattened and the fences blown down. Nearby, large swathes

The aftermath of the 1987 'Great Storm'. Scenes like this covered much of Britain the following morning. *(Courtesy of David Wright/Geograph project)*

of trees had been uprooted and the streets were littered with debris. Across the country an estimated 15 million trees were flattened and many cars were crushed by falling branches. Boats were wrecked and run aground, the rail network ground to a halt and electricity supplies were cut off to several hundred thousand people.

It took some weeks before everything returned to normal but the evidence of the storm can still be seen today in many forests where fallen trees continue to litter the landscape.

Black Monday

Just three days after the Great Storm had abated, an enormous international stock market crash occurred, hitting Hong Kong first then spreading to Europe and eventually the USA. In a very short space of time, the UK stock market fell 26.45 per cent which, although severe, was nothing compared to Hong Kong's 45.5 per cent crash and New Zealand's 60 per cent drop. Black Monday heralded the largest one-day percentage decline ever in the Dow Jones.

I won't attempt to explain the causes of the crash beyond saying that it was most likely caused by something called 'program trading', where computers perform rapid stock executions based on external inputs, such as the price of related securities, and the scale of the crash was escalated by mass panic. I don't pretend to understand the intricacies of the stock market, but I do know that a lot of people lost a lot of money that day, a few people made a lot of money and the repercussions were felt for years to come.

Harrods Bombing

On 17 December 1983 a car bomb exploded outside the Harrods department store in central London, killing six people and injuring ninety others. The bomb contained around 30lb of explosives and was left in a 1972 blue Austin 1300 parked outside the side entrance of Harrods, on Hans Crescent, and was set with a forty-minute timer. At 12:44 a coded warning was given but it took over half an hour for police to arrive on the scene and tragically the bomb detonated just as the police officers approached the car. Three of the officers were killed, along with three passers-by, and ninety other people were injured.

My wife was in London on that fateful day, Christmas shopping with her parents and sister, and they had been into Harrods just a couple of hours previously. After stopping for lunch nearby, they decided to return to Harrods to buy something they had seen earlier. As they walked back along Brompton Road towards the store, they saw a police van speed past and commented to each other on the festive tinsel adorning the radio aerial. Minutes later, as they stood opposite the department store, they heard a tremendous 'dead' bang followed by a moment of shocked silence before people began screaming and running from the scene. It wasn't until later that my wife, aged just 10 at the time, discovered that three of those policemen she had seen race past in their festively decorated van had been killed in the blast.

On every previous visit to London, my wife and her family had always parked their car right outside Harrods in the exact same spot where the bomb had exploded, but on this occasion my wife's mother, a born-again Christian, had said she strongly felt the Lord was telling her not to park there. Not knowing the reason why, but being obedient to their faith, they parked near Hyde Park instead and were spared the disastrous consequences.

Fall of the Berlin Wall

I remember being delighted when the news reports showed the first images of East and West German citizens joining forces to tear down the Berlin Wall in November 1989. As a 12-year-old child I had no real idea what the Berlin Wall was, why it was there, and why it was being torn down, but everyone else seemed to be excited about it so I joined in the celebration.

It wasn't until some time later that I learned the Berlin Wall had been erected in 1961 as a way to completely separate the German Democratic Republic (GDR, East Germany) from the reputedly fascist elements of West Germany. In reality, the wall served to prevent the mass emigration and defection that had seen over 3.5 million East Germans flee into West Berlin during the post-Second World War period.

The tall concrete wall was 96 miles long and heavily guarded with over 300 watchtowers and bunkers; along with the much longer Inner German Border, the wall came to symbolise the Iron Curtain that separated Western Europe and the Eastern bloc during the cold war.

In 1989 a series of radical political changes occurred in the Eastern bloc and after several weeks of civil unrest, the East German government finally announced that all GDR citizens were free to visit West Germany. Crowds of ecstatic East Germans climbed onto the wall and crossed over, joined by West Germans on the other side, and members of the public began to chip away parts of

The fall of the Berlin Wall, November 1989. An East German guard speaks to a West German through a broken seam in the wall. *(Courtesy of Sharon Emerson / Wikimedia Commons)*

the wall with hammers. The governments later removed most of the rest of the wall and within the space of a year German reunification was formally concluded on 3 October 1990.

Live Aid

It is impossible to forget those haunting images of the starving Ethiopian people reported on BBC News by Michael Buerk in 1984. The devastating Ethiopian famine was claiming the lives of hundreds of thousands of men, women and children and many people felt moved to do something to help alleviate the suffering.

Boomtown Rats singer Bob Geldof was one of those people moved by the news reports and after calling in support from Ultravox front man Midge Ure, the pair penned the now-famous song *Do They Know It's Christmas?*. Geldof created a group called Band Aid to record the track which featured many of the most popular British and Irish musicians of the time and when the single was released it shot to number one in the charts, where it stayed for five weeks, generating around £8 million for Ethiopian famine relief.

Following the success of the Band Aid single, Geldof conceived the idea of staging an enormous concert with all the biggest acts in the music business at the time. Although faced with numerous, seemingly impossible obstacles to staging a concert of this magnitude,

Live Aid at JFK Stadium, Philadelphia, 1985. *(Courtesy of Squelle/Wikimedia Commons)*

Geldof managed to persuade dozens of acts to perform for free, and he arranged a live television broadcast that was watched by an estimated 1.9 billion people around the world.

Two concerts were held simultaneously on 13 July 1985, one in Wembley Stadium and the other in the JFK Stadium in Philadelphia. Phil Collins famously performed at both concerts: starting with a gig at Wembley, he was then flown to Heathrow airport by Noel Edmonds in his helicopter to board Concorde. Thanks to the supersonic passenger jet, Collins crossed the Atlantic in time to perform at the Philadelphia concert as well.

Throughout the concerts, television viewers were urged to donate money via the Live Aid phone lines and seven hours into the concert, Geldof asked how much money had been raised. The answer was £1.2 million which reportedly disappointed and angered him and led to him marching to the BBC commentary box to make an appeal. Here he was interviewed by BBC presenter David Hepworth, who attempted to provide a list of addresses to which cheques could be sent, but the passionate Geldof interrupted him in mid-flow and shouted, 'F★★k the address, let's get the numbers!'

By the time Live Aid was concluded, around £150 million had been raised and Geldof received an honorary knighthood for his efforts.

Blue Peter Garden Vandalised

In November 1983 children across the UK sat and watched *Blue Peter* in cross-legged horror as Janet Ellis mournfully confirmed that vandals had broken into the *Blue Peter* garden and wrought terrible destruction. When you consider the magnitude of some of the tragedies that occurred in the eighties, you would be forgiven for thinking that the vandalism of the *Blue Peter* garden was relatively inconsequential, but for the children of our nation this was a tragedy that was very personal to them and was one for which they felt a sense of real outrage.

The vandals, who remain unidentified to this day, broke into the *Blue Peter* compound at Television Centre and smashed the ornamental urn (given to them by Mrs Taylor from Barnett, apparently) and callously threw the sundial into the fish pond, along with some fuel oil which killed a number of the fish. As if that wasn't enough, they also trampled on the bedding plants and tipped over a garden bench.

The entire *Blue Peter* team immediately set to work repairing the damage and were able to save some of the fish, but for poor old Percy Thrower it was all too much, and he had tears in his eyes as he told Janet that the culprits must have been mentally ill.

1984 Summer Olympics

In 1984 I remember watching the opening ceremony of the Los Angeles Olympics with great excitement as a man wearing a jetpack flew around the stadium for a few seconds before landing in the middle, much to the delight of millions of spectators. From this moment on, I was fully expecting to be given my very own child-size jetpack for my birthday or Christmas and was sorely disappointed when the jetpack never arrived. It wasn't until I saw the film *Back to the Future* a couple of years later that my desire to own a jetpack was replaced by my dream of owning a hoverboard, a dream which persists to this day.

The whole jetpack thing is all I really remember from the 1984 Olympics, but apparently there were some sporting events as well, which included the debut appearance of Carl Lewis, who won four gold medals, and saw Sebastian Coe become the first man to win consecutive gold medals in the 1500m having previously won gold in 1980.

In addition to the numerous sporting achievements, the 1984 Olympics were notable for the absence of fourteen Eastern bloc countries, including the Soviet Union who boycotted the Games in retaliation for the US boycott of the previous Soviet Games. The boycott had a dramatic impact, most notably in the weightlifting events where ninety-four of the world's top 100 ranked lifters were absent, along with twenty-nine of the thirty medallists from the recent world championships and all ten of the defending world champions in the ten weight categories.

Despite the boycott, 140 nations participated in the Games with over 6,829 athletes participating in 221 events.

1988 Winter Olympics

While the 1984 Summer Olympics was most memorable, in my opinion, for the jetpack man at the opening ceremony, the 1988 Winter Olympics was most memorable for the debut appearance of the Jamaican bobsleigh team.

The four-man Jamaican bobsleigh team was assembled by two Americans, Fitch and Maloney, who visited Jamaica and witnessed a pushcart derby, which is very similar, in essence, to bobsledding. Knowing that bobsledding was dependent on very quick starts, they selected four fast sprinters to form a team and made their way to Calgary, Alberta, where the Olympics was being held.

Coming from a tropical country, the Jamaican team was something of a novelty and they had little opportunity to practise on a real bobsled track and didn't even have their own bobsled. Fortunately, the other teams lent them spare bobsleds and offered them guidance and support in a show of sporting brotherhood. The team became firm favourites with the spectators, representing the ultimate underdog story in sport.

Despite making excellent progress, the team didn't officially finish after they lost control of the sled during one of the four runs and crashed at over 70mph. After coming to a rest near the finish line, the four men were helped from the sled before walking to the finish line as the crowds cheered them on.

This failure didn't deter the team and they returned to the Games in the 1992 French Winter Olympics and went on to place fourteenth in the 1994 Norwegian Winter Olympics, beating the United States, Russia, Australia, France and one sled from Italy.

The Jamaican bobsleigh team was the inspiration for a major movie in 1992, *Cool Runnings*, in which John Candy starred as the team's coach.

Maradona's 'Hand of God' Goal

Many English football fans still feel deep bitterness and resentment towards the Argentinean football team for the events that took place on 22 June 1986 at the quarter final of the 1986 FIFA World Cup.

Having enjoyed a gradual improvement in form throughout the World Cup, England were ready to take on their old nemesis Argentina in the quarter finals, confident that they could beat them and go on to win the World Cup. Rivalry between England and Argentina ran deep, thanks to a previous falling out at the 1966 World Cup, and tensions were now heightened due to the recent Falklands Conflict, just four years earlier, which had resulted in 258 British and 649 Argentinean deaths.

An uneventful first half saw no goals scored but the second half went on to produce two of the most famous (or infamous) moments in football history. Six minutes into the second half, Argentinean player Diego Maradona punched the ball into the goal with his fist and the referee, not having seen what happened, allowed the illegal goal. It didn't take long before the slow-motion replays confirmed that Maradona had indeed used his hand to score the goal but by that time it was too late and the referee's decision had been made. After the match, Maradona claimed that the goal was scored 'a little with the head of Maradona and a little with the hand of God', leading to the goal being forever known as the 'Hand of God' goal.

Just four minutes after this infamous goal, with the England players and fans still reeling in disbelief at what had just happened, Maradona made an impressive 60-metre dash up the pitch, dribbling the ball past five English outfield players before manoeuvring around the goalkeeper and scoring a second goal. The goal was so impressive that it was later voted 'Goal of the Century' and it was this goal that secured victory for the Argentinean team over England in the quarter finals.

Zeebrugge Ferry Disaster

It was a Friday night and we had just been watching *Blankety Blank* with Les Dawson when the newsflash appeared on the television and Nicholas Witchell told us that a ferry carrying more than 600 people on board had capsized just one mile off the coast of Belgium. The vessel was called the *Herald of Free Enterprise*, part of the Townsend Thoreson fleet, and was on her way from Zeebrugge to Dover. At the time of the newsflash, little information was available other than that the ferry was currently lying on its side and that rescue teams were on their way.

It wasn't until some time later that the full extent of the situation became clear and we learned that 193 people had been killed in the tragedy, mostly as a result of hypothermia from submersion in the icy cold water. Many of those on board had been *Sun* newspaper readers taking advantage of a promotion for cheap trips to the Continent.

The ferry was a roll-on, roll-off vehicle ferry and an investigation after the event concluded that it had capsized due to the bow loading doors being accidentally left open as the ship left the harbour. Water had poured

Seconds after the attempted assassination of Ronald Reagan on 30 March 1981 outside the Washington Hilton Hotel. *(Public Domain)*

into the car deck and rapidly caused the ship to become unstable and capsize within just ninety seconds of the water first entering, without time for the crew to raise the alarm.

Following the disaster, a number of modifications to the design and procedures for roll-on, roll-off ferries were introduced to prevent a similar incident ever happening again.

Chernobyl Disaster

Reactor number four at the Chernobyl nuclear power plant in Ukraine began a systems test on Saturday, 26 April 1986 which recorded a sudden power output surge. An emergency shutdown was attempted but this was followed by an even larger power surge. A reactor vessel ruptured which led to a series of explosions, resulting in the ignition of the graphite moderator. A large plume of highly radioactive smoke rose from the reactor into the atmosphere and spread over an enormous area, causing widespread contamination of the Soviet Union and Europe. Around 50,000 people from the nearby city of Prypiat were immediately evacuated but the contamination was so severe that other towns nearby were also evacuated; in total, over 350,000 people were resettled after the disaster.

It is estimated that thirty-one staff and emergency workers died as a direct result of the accident, but the

World Health Organisation estimated that 4,000 civilians may have been killed some time after the event as a result of radiation exposure. Further studies have suggested that the long-term effects of the incident could ultimately lead to 200,000 premature cancer deaths, although the full impact will probably never be known for certain.

The majority of the radioactive fallout landed in Ukraine and Belarus, but the pollution spread across Europe and contaminated some areas so badly that slaughter restrictions for grazing animals had to be imposed since their meat was considered unsafe for human consumption. As of 2012, restrictions still apply to the slaughter of sheep in some parts of the UK and it is expected that the radioactivity from Chernobyl will be found in the UK and Norway for at least another 100 years.

Christmas

Here's something a little lighter to close the chapter – a happy world event for most – Christmas in the 1980s. The excitement would begin the night before Christmas when my dad would take us out into the garden and we'd all look up at the sky to see if we could see Santa flying around on his sleigh. We never saw anything, of course, but we always managed to convince ourselves that we had. We would leave out milk and a cookie for Santa and a carrot for the reindeer and place a plastic

'Santa sack' at the foot of our beds in the hope that we would find it filled in the morning. After trying to stay awake for as long as possible, we eventually drifted off to sleep and would awake the next morning at some ridiculously early time to noisily wake up our parents and take our Santa sacks into the living room to unpack them, as my dad filmed our reactions with his cine camera.

We knelt on the floor in our picture pyjamas (mine was He-Man) and rummaged through the sacks excitedly, chattering to each other about what gifts we had received. We would usually get a mix of the exciting and the slightly more mundane gifts that ranged from something cool like a Rubik's Cube to something practical like a new pair of socks, or on one occasion a jar of pickled onions. Whatever it was we were given, we would gleefully exclaim, 'just what I always wanted!' and while we were generally very grateful for our gifts, I do remember causing a scene one Christmas after counting up the gifts to discover my brother had been given one more present than me.

On Christmas day 1980 a heavy snowfall covered the country and my dad took the opportunity to add a little magic to the day by sneaking outside and making some reindeer 'hoof prints' in the snow to show us evidence of Santa's nocturnal activity. A little piece of nibbled carrot lay on the ground next to the hoof prints and a set of boot prints led from the flying-sleigh landing area to the back door of the house.

After the presents had been opened, a celebratory breakfast would be prepared which was essentially the same as a normal breakfast but included a glass of Corona Cherryade or Limeade. Suitably refreshed we would begin playing with our new toys as mum busied herself in the kitchen preparing a veritable feast for the Christmas lunch. Sometimes our grandparents would join us, or maybe our great-aunt, and we'd all get together and exchange yet more gifts.

My mum would usually be given some kind of soap, body cream or other beauty lotion, and maybe a sweet treat like a box of Turkish delight or a Walnut Whip. My dad would be given a bottle of Old Spice aftershave and a pack of handkerchiefs. My gran would get a calendar and would always exclaim, 'Oh, you shouldn't have!' at which point the present was jokingly retrieved. My older brother would get a soap-on-a-rope and a Hai Karate talcum powder.

After the presents had been opened, we'd sit up for a spectacular lunch of roast turkey with all the trimmings and the adults would drink Blue Nun, Babycham and egg nog, while the children drank more Corona. We would pull crackers, share jokes and wear silly party hats and then retire in front of the television to watch the Queen's speech. The afternoon would be spent playing with our new toys as the grown-ups talked about boring, grown-up stuff, and by teatime we would all be so worn out from the festivities and excessive sugar consumption that we would happily settle down to watch the Christmas specials of *Morecambe and Wise*, *Only Fools and Horses* or *The Two Ronnies* at the end of a perfect day.

Nine

STREET LIFE

I'm sure you've heard it said before, but whatever happened to white dog poo? Back in the 1980s, every pavement in the country was littered with neat little piles of chalky-white dog poo that was dry and brittle and crunched when you rode over it on your Raleigh Grifter. In those days people fed their dogs bones which contained a high dose of calcium, causing the dogs' poos to be white. Today's dog poos aren't white and neither are they crunchy and brittle. They're brown and stinky and, quite frankly, they're just not the same. I miss white dog poo.

But it's not just the white dog poos I miss, because virtually every area of our lives was different back in the eighties – some things for the better and some for the worse. Apart from fashion, music and TV, we drove different cars, ate different food, shopped at different shops and even decorated our houses differently. The way we spent our leisure time was different, the way we worked was different and even the way we thought was different. I miss it all but I'm not sure I want it all back since I quite like the future, too. If only there was some way of time-travelling so we could go and visit the eighties from time to time.

Well, just imagine for a moment that we've managed to borrow Doc Brown's time-travelling DeLorean from *Back to the Future* because we're going to take a trip back in time to see how different life really was in the 1980s. I've set the flux capacitor to 3 July 1985 (the date *Back to the Future* was released) and I'm going to take you back to the town where I grew up.

On arriving in a blaze of fire in the sleepy Dorset town where I spent my childhood, probably the first difference you would notice is the other cars on the road around you. The majority of cars being driven in the eighties were angular in design and, in my opinion, singularly unattractive having lost some of the pioneering passion and charm of earlier motoring years and now embraced utilitarian and cost-saving designs well suited to modern mass production. This was a time when Skoda was the laughing stock of the automotive world and some of the most popular car colours included rust-brown, mustard-yellow and just plain old beige. And, of course, not everyone had new cars so there was also a significant proportion of clapped-out 1970s cars still on the road.

Not all the cars were hideous and there were a number of notable exceptions such as the lovely Lamborghini

Countach, the fabulous Ferrari Testarossa and the pretty Porsche 959. These cars were so outstandingly beautiful that virtually every young boy in the country had a poster of at least one of them on his bedroom wall; and in extreme cases of limited space, people actually removed their 'tennis girl scratching her bum' poster and replaced it with a picture of a red Ferrari Testarossa. In a rather serendipitous turn of events, the designs of the most popular super cars at the time perfectly complimented the eighties decor of many boys' bedrooms, with their use of striking colours (mainly red, yellow, black or white) and geometric designs that reflected the angular shapes found in the wallpaper patterns.

While some truly astounding cars were being made and sold to yuppies in the eighties, it was actually very rare to see one in the flesh. In everyday driving you were much more likely to pass a slurry-brown Rover 2000 driven by an old man with just his hat visible above the steering wheel than you were to encounter a James Bond

A splendid example of a Ford Capri S coupe. *(Courtesy of OSX/Wikimedia Commons)*

type driving an amphibious Lotus Esprit like the one in *The Spy Who Loved Me*.

If you could see the cars my neighbours drove in the eighties you would see a motley collection of Montegos, Ford Cortinas, Austin Metros, one red Triumph Dolomite and a Rover Princess. In my parents' driveway you would see a sky-blue Datsun Cherry that smelled funny and made me feel carsick, and if my medallion-wearing, hairy-chested next-door neighbour was at home, you would see a bright orange Ford Capri complete with furry dice and a musical Dixie horn like they had in the *Dukes of Hazzard*.

One of our elderly neighbours decided that, instead of having a car, he would join the 17,000 other people in the country who had bought a Sinclair C5, believing it to be a practical and cost-efficient alternative for short journeys. In reality, the C5 was nothing more than a battery-assisted recumbent tricycle dressed with a futuristic-looking plastic outer case; but Clive Sinclair, the inventor, declared that it was going to revolutionise transport around the world. Since Mr Sinclair was seen as something of a visionary after having brought us the ZX80, ZX81 and ZX Spectrum home computers, many people believed the C5 was the next big thing.

The C5, however, was a commercial disaster and was abandoned just months after its initial launch due to poor sales and design problems. Since the C5 was so low to the ground with an open cockpit, it was badly exposed to the weather and was unusable for much of the year thanks

A Sinclair C5 from 1985, just like the one I used to borrow from my elderly neighbour to cruise around the streets in. *(Courtesy of Grant Mitchell/ Wikimedia Commons)*

to the good old British weather; and it quickly became apparent that the motor was completely useless on even the slightest incline meaning that it had to be pedalled up hills to avoid the motor overheating. Quite aside from all of this, the C5 looked ridiculous and made *you* look even more ridiculous as you pedalled it furiously up a hill on a busy main road with a stream of angry motorists stuck behind you shouting abuse.

Every cloud has a silver lining, though, and my brothers and I were delighted when our disappointed neighbour decided that he wasn't going to use his C5 after all and offered it to us to play with as a kind of fancy go-kart. Since the C5 had a maximum speed of 15mph, we didn't need a licence to drive it, so we would spend many happy minutes (not hours, because the battery never lasted that long) whizzing around the quiet residential roads nearby trying in vain to get the C5 to do a wheelie.

On the subject of electric vehicles, a time-traveller to the eighties might also notice what would appear to be a uniformed naval officer driving an open-sided, three-wheeled, battery-powered van, precariously laden with hundreds of bottles of milk. This would be, of course, our local milkman, Barry, who diligently fulfilled the stereotype assigned to milkmen by delivering more than just a bottle of milk to the homes of numerous lonely housewives. Quite why milkmen used to wear uniforms I don't know, but I suspect it may have been at the request of the housewives.

Now, if you were to drive the DeLorean into town you would notice at once the different face of the high street, which was populated with fondly remembered shops such as Ratner's the budget jewellers, John Menzies the newsagents, Bejam the frozen food store, Tandy the electrical store, Our Price the record shop, Do It All the DIY shop, Woolworths the general store and The Sweater Shop which sold, erm … sweaters. If you wanted to buy a television you could go to Rumbelows which was very similar to Comet or Currys, and if you couldn't afford to buy the television outright, you could always rent it, along with a Betamax video recorder, from Radio Rentals next door.

The high street appeared to be thriving, but it was already under threat from the rise of out-of-town supermarkets and popular new shopping centres that housed numerous stores under a single roof. Old Victorian buildings were torn down and replaced with modern concrete shopping centres built in a brutalist style, causing great controversy at the time and still generating an emotional response in many people today. The advantages and attraction of the new shopping centres were obvious, both for shoppers and retailers alike: all the shops were in one place so you didn't have to walk all over town; there were no roads or cars to worry about; you were protected from the weather and there was plenty of car parking right next to the shops.

The most well known of all the shopping centres was probably the Arndale Centre which was actually a collection of twenty-two different shopping centres across the UK, rather confusingly all called the Arndale Centre. Whenever I hear the name, I remember a sketch from the TV show *A Bit of Fry and Laurie*, where Stephen Fry is looking to buy a get-well-soon card for his wife in a shop where the cards have curiously specific messages. He doesn't find the card he wants but does find a card with a message that reads, 'Sorry to hear your teeth fell out in the Arndale Centre, all my love Thomas'.

While the physical structure of the high street was undergoing something of a revolution, another retail revolution was taking place inside the shops as an exciting technology called 'the barcode' began to be used more widely. Although the bar code had been invented many years earlier, it wasn't until the 1970s that it made its debut in the retail environment, and it took many more

years before most retailers adopted the system since it
required an expensive upgrade to their tills and computer
systems. Prior to the bar code retailers used sticky price
labels, marking up the price of each Mars Bar individu-
ally (10p for a Mars Bar in 1980 incidentally), but this was
a laborious process and often led to errors or dishonesty,
with customers swapping price stickers around for their
own benefit. Most people embraced the new technology, which sped up the process of paying for their goods,
but a few conspiracy theorists considered barcodes to be
an intrusive surveillance technology and some Christians
became concerned when they realised that every barcode contains the number 666, apparently fulfilling the
biblical prophecy 'that no one may buy or sell except
one who has the mark or the name of the beast, or the
number of his name … His number is 666'.

After having perused the pleasures of the 1980s high
street you could wander around one of the many supermarkets or grocery stores of the time, like Safeways,
Mainstop, Happy Shopper, Presto or Pricerite, to remind
yourself of the different foods we used to eat in the eighties, and the cheesy muzak that the supermarkets played
for us while we were doing the shopping. Of course,
most of the essentials were just the same as the food we
eat today – meat, fish, dairy, vegetables and so on – but
with a bit less variety. It would have been quite unusual
to see a sweet potato, star fruit or papaya in the shops and
you certainly wouldn't expect to see much in the way of
organic produce.

The eighties was a time when we increasingly looked for time-saving, or convenience foods, and we didn't think so much about what went into the food or what its nutritional value was. There was no labelling on the food to tell you how many calories were in it, no traffic light warnings printed on the pack to show you the fat, sugar and salt content, and even if there had been, we probably wouldn't have paid much attention. The traditional stay-at-home housewife role was rapidly vanishing and being replaced by the new, power-dressing career women that didn't have time to cook long-winded roast dinners, opting to use their brand-new, high-speed microwave ovens instead. In some extreme cases, women stopped cooking altogether and it was reported that men had to cook their own dinner.

Consequently, the supermarkets of the eighties would be full of shoulder-padded women or bewildered men with trolleys full of the new and exciting convenience foods that had only recently appeared on the shelves. Take, for example, the Pot Noodle which appeared in 1979; if you could make a cup of tea, you could make a Pot Noodle – perfect for the unadventurous man whose wife had become a career woman. The manufacturers even targeted their adverts at men to show them just how easy it was to prepare their food in the absence of a woman. According to the adverts for Findus Crispy Pancakes, the pancakes were so easy to prepare that even a teenage boy could manage it while his mum was out at work. The sneaky teenage boy in the advert impressed his girlfriend by letting her think he had fantastic culinary skills and had made the pancakes from scratch, when in actual fact, he had just taken them out of the freezer and put them in the oven.

If you wanted potato with your meal, you didn't need to scrub and peel real potatoes; you just added some hot water to Smash or chucked a couple of the brand-new Bird's Eye Potato Waffles in the oven. For dessert, you could just add water again to a packet of butterscotch Angel Delight, or maybe, if you had guests, you could bring out the latest innovation in ice cream: the Vienetta.

What would be the perfect drink to accompany this 1980s convenience meal? Why, Blue Nun of course! Blue Nun was famously marketed as the wine that would accompany every meal perfectly, reducing the need for complicated wine pairings between courses and shaving vital seconds off mealtime preparation. If you preferred something non-alcoholic you could always open a can of TAB Clear cola, the colourless, sugarless cola that never really made it big; or maybe you could open that bottle of Corona limeade that the Corona man delivered to your doorstep every week.

Shoppers at a 1980s supermarket would take their goods to the tabard-wearing checkout assistant who would tap the prices into the till manually, fingers fast as lightning, pausing occasionally to hold up an embarrassing item which had lost its sticky price label and call out for a 'price check'. Credit cards were becoming more widely used to pay for goods on the high street but they were still relatively new and mistrusted by many. Most customers still opted to pay for their goods with 'real money', like £1 notes, old-fashioned shillings, and maybe even some ha'penny coins up until 1984.

I didn't do a lot of supermarket shopping in 1985 since I was just 8 years old and I was a lot more familiar with a different type of shop – the sweet shop. I used to be given 20p pocket money each weekend and as soon as I got it, I would rush off to the corner shop and spend the whole lot on a big bag of sweets. Items to choose from were things like Alphabet Candy, Beer Bottles, Cola Bottles, Anglo Bubble Gum, Candy Necklaces, Eyeball Gobstoppers, Space Dust, Candy Cigarettes, Bazooka Joe Bubble Gum, Skull Crushers, Flumps, Bullion Bars, Flying Saucers, Cola Roller Balls, Fireball Gobstoppers, Foam Magic Mushrooms, Gold Rush Bubble Gum, Horror Bags, Jaw Breakers, Mojos, Blackjacks, Fruit Salads, Parma Violets, Pez, Love Hearts, Pink Shrimps, Sherbet Dip Dabs or Fountains, Rainbow Drops and Wham Bars.

The corner shop also stocked a mouth-watering selection of crisps, including Ringos, Fish and Chips, Space Raiders, Scampi Fries, Piglets, Discos, Monster Munch and, my personal favourite, the highly controversial hedgehog-flavoured crisps. In 1981 a Welsh pub owner called Philip Lewis decided, as something of a joke, to invent hedgehog-flavoured crisps and was as surprised as everyone else when the crisps became enormously

An original packet of hedgehog-flavoured crisps from 1981. This packet dates from just before the court case which resulted in the name of the crisps being changed ever so slightly to 'hedgehog flavour', instead of 'hedgehog flavoured'. *(Public Domain)*

successful. He was also surprised when the Office of Fair Trading decided to bring a court case against him for false advertising, since they weren't happy when they discovered that the crisps did not actually contain any hedgehogs at all. Mr Lewis explained that he had interviewed travelling gypsies, who enjoyed the occasional baked hedgehog or two, and took their advice on the flavourings required to recreate the authentic flavour of baked hedgehog. Well, to cut a long story short,

Mr Lewis simply changed the label on the packet to read 'hedgehog flavour' instead of 'hedgehog flavoured', and everyone was happy again.

Once we had stocked up on our sweets and snacks, my brothers and I would head back home in silence, unable to speak thanks to the giant gobstoppers crammed in our mouths. At the weekends we would usually meet up with our friends and spend the whole time playing in the street on our skateboards, setting up makeshift ramps and using them to jump over brave 'volunteers' (usually me) lying on the ground underneath. This was no sissy 1970s skateboarding, where the tricks involved girly handstands and stationary acrobatics while flare-wearing onlookers declared your tricks to be 'wizard'; no, this was 1980s street skating and we weren't 'wizard', we were 'radical'. We were part of a new movement of gritty, urban skaters popularised by skateboarding magazines like *Thrasher* and *R.A.D.* (Read and Destroy). We would ollie, grind and rail-slide around the streets emulating our heroes, the famous skaters Tony Hawk, Steve Caballero and Rodney Mullen. We watched skate videos together, we read skate magazines and we even played skating computer games like 'Skate or Die' on the ZX Spectrum. The only problem was that I was no good at it. I couldn't ollie to save my life and when I was towed behind a bike on my skateboard I got the speed wobbles, fell off and ended up in hospital.

When a friend of mine brought a skateboard into the office recently, all the excitement of the eighties came

Me getting totally radical at the local skate park. *(Author's Collection)*

flooding back to me and we decided to take it for a whizz down the hill nearby. I'd completely forgotten that I was no longer a child and that I was never much good at skateboarding anyway, and so it came as something of a surprise when I came flying off the skateboard at great speed, landing on my face and ending up covered in bandages once more.

A marginally safer activity was riding our bicycles, although we still received our fair share of cuts, bruises and crossbar-induced testicular concussions. My brother had a bright yellow Mongoose BMX and I had a Raleigh Grifter that was so heavy that it felt like it was made of lead. The Grifter was the younger cousin of the Raleigh Chopper, a seventies cultural icon, and it looked like the sort of sporty BMX bike that would be ideal for performing stunts and tricks. However, it weighed in at around 35lb making it far too heavy for any child to ever do any jumps on it, which was probably just as well with my safety record. Instead of attempting to get airborne on the bike, I would Sellotape some Brooke Bond PG Tip tea cards on to the frame, sticking into the spokes, so that as I rode along, the cards flapped against the spokes and made a kind of 'vroom' noise like a motorbike. At my request my dad bought me a rear-view mirror for the bike and, when combined with the 'vroom' noise from the spokes, the twist shift gears and the excessive weight of the bike, I was able to pretend I was one of the motorbike-riding characters from CHiPs.

My younger brother would join in and pretend he was on a police motorbike as he rode around on his Raleigh Bluebird, a younger child's bike that had a sky-blue frame, white tyres, a white saddle and white handle grips. It came equipped with stabilisers and a little carry box mounted on the rear mudguard that came in handy for transporting our toy handcuffs and revolver.

Sometimes we would head up to the woods on our bikes where someone had made a kind of dirt racetrack with hard-packed mounds of earth that acted as ramps and obstacles. My brother, on his lightweight Mongoose BMX, would speed around the track clearing every obstacle with ease, soaring gracefully through the air over the various ramps. I would follow on my super-heavy Grifter, ploughing through the obstacles with sheer, unstoppable momentum before attempting one of the ramps; my weighty bike always remained firmly rooted to the ground while I soared gracefully through the air, just like my brother, except without a bike.

Just next to the dirt track in the woods was the local Scout hut where my brother and I went once a week for Cub Scouts. We would dress in the traditional Cub's uniform of grey shorts, green jumper, green cap and a striped neck scarf, with a red 'woggle' to fasten the scarf. We also had to wear green-tabbed garters around our knee-length grey socks.

Each week we would solemnly declare our oath to Akela and give a three-fingered salute as the Union Jack flag was raised on a piece of string indoors (we didn't have a flagpole to use outside). Aside from the weekly meetings where we learnt to tie knots, start fires and practise basic first aid, we would occasionally be taken on special outings or would take part in activities that earned us badges that we could proudly stitch onto the sleeves of our jumpers. Once a year, we would take part in 'Bob-a-Job' week which involved knocking on the doors of neighbours and asking if they had any odd jobs we could do to earn some money. Bob-a-Job week started just after the Second World War and the participating Scouts would be paid 5p per job ('bob' is the old name for a shilling, now 5p), but in the 1980s inflation meant that I could charge up to 50p per job. This was no easy money-making scheme, though, and I would be expected to work hard for my 50p. I remember weeding an elderly neighbour's garden for over an hour to earn 50p, washing my dad's car to gleaming perfection for another 50p and cutting another neighbour's enormous lawn with a heavy old-fashioned mower for another 50p. Frustratingly, all the money I had worked so hard to collect had to be given to the Scouts for their fundraising collection and I never got to keep a penny of it. I think the idea was to teach young boys the value of voluntary service and community spirit, but it taught me a different lesson: that hard work was futile and that community spirit meant giving up your weekends so that elderly neighbours could take advantage of your good nature.

I worked pretty hard over the years to raise money for the Scouts as I would also go door-to-door each week with a wheelbarrow collecting stacks of old newspapers to take to the Scout hall so they could sell the paper for recycling. I reckon the Scouts did pretty well out of me.

Well, it's been a real pleasure showing you around my home town of the 1980s and I hope it has brought back as many good memories for you as it has for me; but now it's time to move on and take a look at what it was like going to school in the eighties.

Ten

SKOOL DAZE

Remember that old ZX Spectrum computer game 'Skool Daze' from 1985? Well, I never really figured out what I was meant to be doing in that game – I guess I just never read the instructions – and so I spent many happy hours guiding my character Eric aimlessly from classroom to classroom with the vague feeling that I was probably in the wrong lesson at the wrong time, and occasionally getting told off by teachers whose names I didn't know. And in this respect 'Skool Daze' bore a remarkable similarity to my own, real-life experience of attending school in the 1980s.

I should preface this chapter of nostalgic school day ramblings by acknowledging that school in the 1980s was undoubtedly a different experience for every child and that each person will have a unique memory of their student years. I would be mightily surprised, however, if you don't find my memories of school life awakening recollections of similar teachers and incidents in your own school days. Of course, many elements of school life will always be the same and children of any generation will share similar experiences, but schooling in the eighties brought with it some unique technologies, trends and events that set it apart from any other decade. I'd like to share with you my personal experience of being a school child in the eighties.

My first day at school is etched indelibly into my memory: it was a sunny September morning in 1982 and my mum held my hand as I walked into the classroom, satchel on my back. Much to my embarrassment, as I walked in through the doorway I tripped on the threshold and landed flat on my face in front of all the assembled children. Not a great start to my school days, but it makes quite a good chapter-opener. Had I known then that I would someday use this experience in a book I was going to write, I might not have cried so much.

My first school was a typical 1970s-built, grey brick box with a large playground and even larger playing field. The playground was split on two levels with a lower playground that was just a rectangle of tarmac and an upper playground that featured a tantalising array of climbing frames and play equipment. I say 'tantalising' because we were never actually allowed to play on the equipment during the whole time I was at the school. Every break time all the children would file past the play equipment looking longingly at the ladders, monkey bars and climbing frames as they made their way to the lower playground. On one occasion, the temptation became too much to resist and a spontaneous rebellion broke out among the children as they rushed on to the play equipment, screaming and shouting with joy. I was among those sent to the headmaster for illegally playing on the climbing frames and to this day I have no idea why we were never allowed to use them.

I'm sure, at some point, someone must have explained to me what school was all about and why I was there, but for some reason it never sunk in. I simply followed my instructions and did what the grown-ups told me without questioning anything. I dutifully made crocodiles out of egg cartons, painted pictures of my parents and glued glitter on to an array of household objects, and for all I knew or cared I could have been part of a child slavery production line manufacturing goods to be sold on the black market.

If we weren't making stuff we were listening to stories or watching some kind of semi-educational children's programme like *Puddle Lane* on an enormous wood-panelled television. The teacher would wheel the television in as the children sat cross-legged on the carpet in excited anticipation and would then spend the next fifteen minutes or so trying to work out how to switch it on. I'm certain a good portion of my school life was spent watching teachers trying to get educational videos to play on Betamax video cassette players.

On Friday afternoons we had 'free time', which was the highlight of the week, when we were allowed to play inside or outside with any of the sports equipment,

A rare Betamax TV/VCR combo, the stuff of nightmares for many school teachers who struggled with any form of new technology. *(Courtesy of Franny Wentzel/Wikimedia Commons)*

games, toys or musical instruments. I liked to go into the Quiet Room on my own with a little electronics set that consisted of a few wires, a light bulb and a battery. When any other children came in to the same room and disturbed me I would tell them I was making a bomb and showed them the sinister-looking tangle of wires and dimly glowing light bulb. I remember one child being quite worried about this and they ran out of the room shouting for the teacher.

At lunchtime all the children would file into the school hall to eat their packed lunches together. As a child from a low-income family, I would hand over my special pink ticket and be given a government-provided packed lunch. The packed lunch was so outstandingly horrible that I can remember the exact contents to this day: soggy sandwiches filled with some kind of grey, bad-tasting reconstituted meat (my brother told me it was donkey meat), a packet of cheese biscuits, a puckered and bruised apple that had definitely seen better days and some kind of dry biscuit with one half dipped in something that looked like chocolate but didn't taste like it. It was virtually the same lunch every day with the only difference being a variation in the unrecognisable meats. After a while I became so sick of the lunches that I stopped eating them altogether and began smuggling them out of the dining hall so I could hide them down the back of the benches in the cloakroom. After some weeks of successfully getting away with this, the school caretaker finally caught me and reported me to the teachers. I was handed back the stockpile of mouldy sandwiches and told to put them out for the birds on the school bird table. To this day I pity the poor unsuspecting chaffinch that discovered my rotten sandwiches.

Even though I didn't enjoy my school lunches, I was one of the few children that enjoyed the milk that we were all encouraged (forced) to drink at break times. Every child was given a miniature glass bottle of milk with a straw in it and told to drink up the lukewarm milk. If you didn't drink up all your milk then you didn't go out to play. The daily milk ritual started at playschool and continued throughout first school and then middle school, and all the while I was told how good it was for me. If I ever had any doubts about whether or not I really needed to drink so much milk, regular television adverts starring Kevin Keegan would be shown in the early afternoon and evening telling me I should drink even more milk and that it was really good for my health.

The health of school children was taken very seriously in the eighties and as well as being given our daily bottle of milk, we were regularly inspected by a variety of nurses and doctors to check that we were healthy in every respect. We started with the nit nurse who would check our heads for any sign of the dreaded head louse, and some weeks later we would see another nurse who would check our hearing and eyesight. Then came the school dentist, who would perform a cursory examination of our mouths, and another nurse would check our height and weight. Whenever the medical van came to the school, the excited chatter among the children would begin and everyone would speculate about what kind of procedure we would be subject to today. Mostly the talk was of large needles and full-body examinations, but fortunately none of the wild rumours turned out to be true. I got a clean bill of health in every examination, probably because I always drank up my milk.

For my final year of first school I was transferred to a different local school because my parents were concerned about the unusual methods of corporal punishment being used, which I seem to remember included pulling children up by their ears. Corporal punishment was not abolished in UK state schools until 1986 and I remember getting a smacked bottom on at least one occasion at first school, probably with very good reason. I think my parents also felt that teachers smoking during lessons was a bad idea.

My next school was set on the top of a hill and nestled in among a perimeter of tall pine trees. The school was split in two with the original Victorian building on one side of the road and a new school and playing field on the other side, consisting mainly of portable buildings, some with the wheels still attached, making them look rather like lorry trailers. My new class was in one such portable building which wobbled, creaked and groaned when anyone walked around in it.

At my new school I suffered, for the first time, the horrendous experience of swimming in an unheated outdoor swimming pool. To this day I shudder at the thought of jumping into the icy water and having to keep swimming just to prevent the onset of hypothermia. Even on a sunny day the pool was bitterly cold because it was shaded by the tall pine trees surrounding it. Everyone had to swim – no exceptions and no excuses. If you forgot to bring your swimming things, the teacher would wait until everyone else had left the pool and make you go in on your own wearing nothing but your pants. We were taught how to swim and dive and sometimes the teacher would throw a handful of coins into the pool and ask us to rescue them for her. It wasn't a great incentive, though, since she always asked for the coins back afterwards and carefully counted them to make sure no one had robbed her.

Back in the relative warmth and comfort of the classroom, our class topic was space travel and we spent a lot of time discussing how the Space Shuttle worked. We even went so far as to create a model Space Shuttle with a balloon propulsion system that whizzed across the classroom on a piece of string. The project was tied in closely with the forthcoming launch of the Space Shuttle Challenger, which was due to take off on Tuesday, 28 January 1986 with seven astronauts on board. Our class was especially interested in this Shuttle launch since one of the crew was a young female school teacher, Christa McAuliffe, who was the first to be selected through Ronald Reagan's Teacher in Space Project designed to inspire students in all things scientific and astronomical.

On the day of the launch, the excitement of the children in our class was barely containable and we could hardly wait to get home from school to watch the Shuttle launch on television. Finally, just before 5 p.m. that evening, we tuned in to BBC1 and waited excitedly as Philip Schofield handed us over to Roger Finn in the *Newsround* studio. *Newsround* opened with the following words: 'Disaster for the Shuttle, an explosion on Challenger' spoken in a very grave voice as we watched video footage of the Space Shuttle disintegrating into a

The disintegration of the Space Shuttle Challenger in 1986. I watched the footage with shocked horror on *John Craven's Newsround*. *(Public Domain)*

terrifying plume of smoke and debris. The camera then cut to a solemn-looking Roger Finn who continued: 'Within the last few minutes we've heard there's been an explosion on board the Space Shuttle Challenger.'

We eventually learned that all seven crew members of the Space Shuttle Challenger, including teacher Christa McAuliffe, had been killed in the disaster which was caused by a faulty O-ring seal on the right solid rocket booster. I remember the terrible feeling of horror, disbelief and grief as we heard about the tragedy which curtailed not only our own school space project, but also led to Ronald Reagan's cancellation of the Teacher in Space Project. Until this point, I had dreamed of becoming an astronaut and often imagined what it would be like to sit in the cockpit of the Space Shuttle, strapped in firmly as the enormous rockets blasted me into outer space. After the Challenger disaster I decided that I would become a fighter pilot instead – a much safer option in my mind.

With our Space Shuttle project firmly behind us, we moved on to new topics, including, rather randomly, basket weaving for which I showed a real flair and great enthusiasm. My parents were initially thrilled with the woven tea tray I brought home but I felt their enthusiasm begin to wane as I continued to bring home more and more woven objects, and each had to be paid for. I remember my teacher suggesting I slow down the pace of production since I was working my way through an alarming amount of materials leaving very little for the other children to use. Fortunately, the basket-weaving lessons were short-lived, most likely because I had used up all the resources, and so we moved on to our next endeavour – learning to play the recorder.

As a class we had already mastered the tambourine, maracas and glockenspiel, and the obvious next step was to take on the challenge of the recorder. For some reason, children of many generations have been forced to learn this bizarre instrument which is rarely heard outside of the English classroom. Looking back, I pity our poor teachers who must have had the patience of saints as they spent countless hours trying to get our class to perform a flawless round of *Frère Jacques* or *Oranges and Lemons*, instead receiving an earful of tuneless screeching.

Every now and again we would be taken on an outing to the zoo, museum or seaside and we would all file on to a dated-looking orange and brown coach that was driven by a worryingly tired and harassed-looking driver. The school coaches invariably smelled of urine and vomit and had chewing gum on the seats and crude anatomical drawings scratched into the windows. Within five minutes of departure, one of the children would start to feel sick, while another child would have a nose bleed. After ten minutes, the first child would vomit over the child next to them and another child would suddenly decide they were bursting for a wee. A fourth child would then spill their orange juice on the floor, while the remaining children sang *The Wheels on the Bus* repeatedly until we reached our destination, only pausing occasionally to ask if we were nearly there yet.

On arriving at our destination, the teacher would count us off the coach only to discover there was an extra child from a different class that wasn't meant to be there. Meanwhile, nose-bleed child, blood splattered down the front of their pristine white shirt, fainted because they were too hot and hungry. We would eventually make our way inside the zoo/museum and be given a clipboard and blunt pencil each so that we could answer some kind of worksheet; inevitably all the pencils would be lost by the time we had reached the first item on the sheet. By this time the rain would usually have started so the emergency cagoules were handed out and since more children were now feeling faint, we'd adjourn for lunch.

I obviously had my, somewhat industrial, government-issue packed lunch with donkey-meat sandwiches and would look on longingly as other children enjoyed a chocolate-spread sandwich, a packet of Ringos, a can of cherry Coke, a packet of raisins and a square of jelly. The warm can of cherry Coke would usually detonate upon opening, covering several children in a fountain of pink foam and leaving more pristine white school shirts ruined.

Having visited the remaining items on the worksheet, we would then head off to the gift shop which was the highlight of the day. Each child had a small amount of spending money, usually kept in some kind of purse or container on a string around their neck, which would be spent on scented erasers, polished stones, coloured sand or leather bookmarks with the name of the attraction printed on them. The children would be counted back on to the coach and the return journey would begin as vomit-child and nose-bleed child began to perform vigorously once more. At some point on the way back the coach would come to a screeching halt as a panicked teacher suddenly realised that the extra child from the other class was still in the gift shop.

Now you may think I am exaggerating with my description of school day trips, but I can honestly say that virtually everything I have described above actually happened, although it probably didn't all take place on the same day.

My time at first school drew to a welcome close and in September 1986, after the seemingly endless summer holidays, I began middle school where I was destined to spend the remainder of the 1980s. Everything was different here: the teachers, the children, the lessons, even the playground games. I had only just settled into the swing of things at my first school, and now I was wrenched from my cosy classroom where I was one of the big kids and thrown into a school where the biggest children had body hair, and one hormonally active child had already begun to grow facial hair.

At the first school, our uniform had been pretty simple and casual: boys wore a blue shirt and the girls wore a blue dress. It didn't really matter what type of shirt or dress it was, as long as it was mainly blue. Or white. And the boys had to wear grey shorts, or black shorts, or trousers. There was just one boy in our class who wore a blue and white striped tie that may or may not have been part of the uniform – no one really knew.

At the middle school, however, our uniform was a lot more disciplined and we had to wear black shoes, black trousers, black jumper, a white shirt and a black and white striped tie. For some reason, my parents decided to embellish upon this uniform by providing me with a

Ready for my first day at 'big school' dressed in a blazer that wasn't part of the uniform and wearing burgundy-coloured loafers with a free Midland Bank school bag. *(Author's Collection)*

black blazer to wear, which wasn't part of the uniform and didn't help me fit in at the school, especially since I was already looking distinctly odd wearing a pair of burgundy loafers and sometimes carrying a briefcase instead of a school bag. Fortunately, I managed to persuade my parents that the blazer was overkill and the burgundy loafers were toned down with the liberal use of some black shoe polish.

Now that we were at middle school we had proper science lessons with Bunsen burners and test tubes, we had geography lessons that taught us about oxbow lakes and plate tectonics, and we learnt about the effects of smoking and how to 'Just Say No' to drug pushers. I felt like a character from *Grange Hill*, but not one of the cool kids like Tucker, more like one of the nerdy ones that got pushed over in the corridor and had no idea where they were meant to be going and which class they were meant to be in. In fact, I remember sitting in the wrong lesson on more than one occasion with the dawning realisation that I didn't recognise any of the other children in the room. Sometimes I sat through the whole of the wrong lesson, having no idea where else I should go, and on other occasions the teacher would spot me and send me on my way, leaving me wandering the corridors peering hopefully through the windows of the other classes looking for faces I recognised.

After finally locating the correct classroom, I was introduced to the exciting new concept of French lessons which taught us essential phrases and vocabulary to prepare us for a future cosmopolitan lifestyle. We were aided in our learning by the ever-popular textbooks called Tricolore, which featured a collection of French stereotypes living in La Rochelle on the west coast of France. The central characters were the Dhome family, who had a baker's shop in the town, and they and their friends would most commonly be found in a local cafe ordering Orangina and ice creams and taking part in various vocabulary-expanding activities. As well as their somewhat unusual passion for Orangina, many of the characters in the Tricolore textbook were prolific letter-writers and liked to tell you all about themselves in writing.

Perhaps the best part of learning French was the role play sessions where we got to pretend that we were grown-ups on holiday in France with the exciting opportunity of ordering beer in a restaurant and being 'married' to the girl at the next desk.

One of the most welcome benefits of my transition to middle school was not having to eat the government-issue packed lunch since my new school had its own canteen staffed by a vast horde of cheery (and some not so cheery) dinner ladies. For the first time I was allowed to choose what I had for lunch and although I still had the low-income pink ticket, this could now be traded for food up to the value of 70p, which back in the mid-1980s was enough to buy you a three-course meal and a carton of milk. From what I understand, the majority of people do not have particularly fond memories of school dinners, but in comparison to the donkey-meat sandwiches

I had endured for the previous four years, the canteen food was manna from heaven. Now I could (and did) order jacket potato with chips and a bag of crisps with a chocolate biscuit for dessert.

After we'd eaten lunch, the dinner ladies would usher us out into the playground for some fresh air and exercise, while a few of the more mischievous children would sneak back into the classrooms and hide to avoid going outside. We would often spend the whole lunchtime just peeking out from under a pile of bags and coats in the coat racks, occasionally ducking for cover to avoid the military patrols of the dinner ladies.

One of the dinner ladies once found herself rooted to the spot in the playground, completely unable to move, after discovering a condom on the ground. Thinking quickly she put her foot on it to hide it from the children and hoped to avoid drawing attention to it. Unfortunately, one eagle-eyed child had already spotted it and word quickly spread around the playground with the result being that within a few minutes, the dinner lady was surrounded by a crowd of inquisitive children asking her what was under her foot, what a condom was and why was she hiding it from them. Without any means of communicating her predicament to other members of staff, she remained in place for the majority of the lunch hour, red-faced and flustered trying to field a barrage of awkward questions.

When we weren't menacing the dinner ladies we took part in normal playground activities for our age group:

some children played ball games, others played chase, and a few others pretended they were lorries and spent the whole time 'driving' around the perimeter of the playground stopping occasionally to load or unload some new cargo. Another group of children battled it out with Top Trumps, while others traded Garbage Pail Kid stickers.

For those of you who have forgotten or blotted out the memory of Garbage Pail Kids, let me take a moment to remind you of them in all their disgusting glory. In 1985 the Topps Company began selling trading card stickers that were a parody of the hugely popular Cabbage Patch Kids. Each trading card featured a different Garbage Pail Kid with some kind of amusing wordplay name like 'Adam Bomb' accompanied by an illustration of the character usually in some kind of revolting scenario involving bodily functions or untimely deaths. The aforementioned example, Adam Bomb, was pictured sat on the floor pressing a detonator button as the top of his head exploded, revealing a mushroom cloud emanating from his skull. The Garbage Pail Kids gained enormous popularity very quickly and were traded in the playground for swapsies, for other toys or even for hard cash. Within a short space of time the craze had become an epidemic that swept the country and was ultimately banned from many schools because of both its unpleasant nature and the distraction it was causing.

Another short-lived playground craze saw nearly every child in the school practising their yo-yo skills with Coca-Cola-branded Russell Spinners, performing special tricks such as the Round the World, Walk the Dog and Rock the Baby. Coca-Cola had been using yo-yos, or spinners as they were otherwise known, as part of a worldwide advertising campaign for many years, but in 1989 a ten-week campaign in the UK resulted in sales of over 4 million Coca-Cola spinners. Red blazer-wearing spinner demonstrators started appearing in schools and shopping centres showing off their skills to the children, sometimes using two spinners simultaneously for extra coolness. Strangely, as children, we thought the demonstrators were cool despite the fact that they were often bearded, overweight, middle-aged men wearing dodgy-looking Butlinesque nylon blazers.

Every newsagent in the country now had at least one big promotional bin full of spinners and spare spinner strings for sale with instruction books on how to perform various tricks and posters advertising the forthcoming Spinner Championships. Over 15,000 competitions were held in high streets and shopping centres in every major town in Great Britain, with over 250,000 children taking part and ending with the National Finals, hosted by Jeremy Beadle at Alton Towers on 8 July 1989.

The yo-yo/spinner craze was short-lived and before long we went back to our traditional games of chasing people, kicking balls, chasing balls and kicking people. The playground games were usually punctuated with messages sent to and from the girls asking the boys who they fancied and if they wanted to 'go out with them'. Sadly, I spent a lot more time being the messenger telling the girls who the boys fancied than being asked out myself. Dating for most of the children was a relatively new concept and I think few of us understood what was required or expected of us and so the majority of 'couples' just expressed their admiration for each other through a messenger, such as me, and then giggled when they saw each other. This would usually continue for a period of several weeks without any actual date taking place and, in most cases, without the 'couple' even speaking to each other. The relationship would often end in tears when one party decided they fancied someone else and would use the messenger (me again) to tell them they were now dumped.

Gradually, we started to get the hang of the dating game and before long some of the boys were holding hands with the girls and the girls began making the boys friendship bracelets. I wanted to get myself a girlfriend and so I worked on making myself more presentable. I began to wash myself more frequently using my Christmas gift soap-on-a-rope, added a liberal dusting of Hai Karate talcum powder and splashed on some of my dad's Old Spice aftershave. I instantly became irresistible to women and attracted the interest of the prettiest girl in the class who agreed to go out with me after a lot of persuasion. The relationship was beautiful while it lasted, but alas, our love was short-lived and after just ten seconds, with no explanation, she said, 'You're dumped.' Still, I could tell all my friends that I had dated the most popular girl in school and, no matter how brief the relationship, that was enough to put a very happy ending on my school days in the eighties.

As I look back at my experience of school in the eighties and compare it to the experiences of my two daughters today, I realise that there are a lot of similarities. Schools in any decade will have eccentric teachers, playground crazes and glockenspiel lessons. Children will always write 58008 on their calculators and then turn them upside down and giggle, and teachers will always know less about new technology than the pupils they are trying to teach it to. But there was something very special and distinctive about school in the eighties; something that cannot ever be recreated, cannot be preserved and can only be remembered by those who were actually there. It was a potent mix of the music, the movies and the fashions of the decade that influenced the way we thought, behaved and dressed. The atmosphere of the time was charged with politics and world events that we'll never see the likes of again, and the technologies we thought were so advanced at the time have disappeared into history forever, replaced by new technologies we could never have dreamed would be possible.

Nowadays, when I play that old ZX Spectrum game 'Skool Daze' on my super-fast modern PC, I still have no idea what I'm doing, where I'm meant to be or what the point of the game is. But, you know what I realised? It doesn't matter because I made it through the real thing.